D0198825

──蒼穹のファフナー──
FAFNER
Dead Aggressor

Written By
Tow Ubukata

Shortly after a prestigious debut winning the Kadokawa Sneaker Grand Prize, the occasionally outrageous Ubukata entered a contract with a game-developing company. In addition to writing novels, Ubukata is involved in the manga, video game, and anime industries. After winning the Japan Science Fiction Grand Prize, this upstart went on to write a straightforward historical novel. Ubukata was also writer for the anime and CD drama of this work.

Color Illustrations By
Hisashi Hirai

An animator by trade, Hirai also does illustrations, manga, and character and mecha designs for video games. He was chief character designer for "Soukyuu no Fafner."

―― 蒼穹のファフナー ――

FAFNER
Dead Aggressor

Written by
TOW UBUKATA

Illustrations by
HISASHI HIRAI

English translation by
Translation By Design

DMP
**DIGITAL MANGA
PUBLISHING**
Los Angeles

FAFNER: DEAD AGGRESSOR

Written by Tow Ubukata
Illustrated by Hisashi Hirai
English translation by Translation By Design

English Edition Published by:
DIGITAL MANGA PUBLISHING
A division of DIGITAL MANGA, Inc.
1487 W 178th Street, Suite 300
Gardena, CA 90248
USA
www.dmpbooks.com
www.junemanga.com

Library of Congress Cataloging-in-Publication Data Available Upon Request

First Edition: July 2008
ISBN-13: 978-1-56970-820-0
10 9 8 7 6 5 4 3 2 1

Printed in China

Contents

Maya Tomi

A childhood friend of Kazuki
Soshi's, Maya is an active girl
an interest in rock climbing.
regarded as a stable young gir
is a late bloomer in matters rom
Though the second daughter
family of doctors, she can't
wrap a bandage.

遠見真矢

Shoko Hazama

Maya's close friend. Plagued with
physical weakness from birth, she is
often absent from school. She never
leaves home without her straw hat.
She longs for Kazuki, and although
this is known to Maya, Shoko has yet
to muster the courage to tell Kazuki,
himself.

羽佐間翔子

A gentle boy, well-liked by all. He
has feelings for Shoko that he i
unable to express. He eventuall
becomes the pilot of the Fafne
Mark Vier, casting himself into
cruel fate.

春日井甲

Koyo Kasugai

CH

pted by the Minashiro family,
n, together with Soshi, learns
ne secret of the island and the
d. She has an earnest character
approaches all matters seriously,
is also plagued by a lack of a
se of self-worth.

蔵前果林

Karin Kuramae

Fafner Mark Elf

A giant humanoid war machine developed by
mankind. The Fafners developed on Tatsumiya Island
are known as Nothung model units and, depending
on the potential of the pilot, are capable of exhibiting
immense power. The name FAFNER refers to the
character in Norse mythology who turned into a
dragon to protect a treasure trove.

RACTERS

Kazuki Makabe

真壁一騎

A young man living with his father, Fumihiko, on Tatsumiya Island. Due to events that occurred during his childhood, he is hesitant to form close relationships with others. The bearer of unrivaled athletic ability, he also excels in cooking and other domestic pursuits. He becomes the pilot of the Fafner Mark Elf after a sudden Festum attack.

Soshi Minashiro

皆城総士

Cool-tempered and popular, Soshi often finds himself in spotlight amongst the youthful inhabitants of the island. Th is a large, noticeable scar running from his eye to his ch Once a close friend of Kazuki's, a past event now keeps t at arm's length. He is the only one capable of operating Siegfried System, which links with Fafner's units' senses

Age fifteen, spring—the beginning of the war.
We were all just there.

Prologue
Noise

It's a vague memory.

Seven, maybe eight children gathered together at what was probably Camphor Park, judging from the one big camphor tree growing there. I don't remember exactly how many children were there. I just remember that among those present were a few that are still fairly close even now, seven years later.

There are things that I can somehow manage to piece back together.

Everyone's serious, hope-filled faces.

I remember the subject of our collective gaze was an old, silver-colored radio.

"I fixed it. It's my radio," someone was saying. In reality, he had found it on the ground near the trash dump on the northern part of the island. But to us at the time, the fact that he had actually fixed the radio himself was something of—or rather, *quite*—a feat. And the fact that priority goes to the one capable of great feats is one thing that hasn't changed. It was his radio.

"That's amazing!"

"Wow!"

The children shouted their praise, trying to take some part in the excitement. Everyone had been thoroughly captivated by this radio. Or, to be more specific, by the noise emanating from it.

"Hey, didja really hear it?"

"I heard it, I tell you. It'll come back eventually."

"Shh. Put a sock in it."

"Hey, won't we be able to hear it if you move this button?"

"Don't touch it. It was just like this when I heard it before."

We remained that way, our ears leaned into the radio for an hour, possibly longer, just listening to that sound of noise like someone chewing on sand. Hoping to hear something echoing between the gaps.

"It's a beautiful voice. So pretty..." someone sighed.

The children were gripped by the feeling that if they didn't hear this "beautiful voice," they'd see the day that they regretted it. It was a rare taste of exhilaration on an island mostly devoid of amusements. That much was certain. We couldn't pass up the opportunity to experience that sensation together. Moreoever, I think we all probably knew this would become a "hot topic" later on. Indeed, at the time it seemed likely to become the greatest subject of discussion we had ever known. Whenever there was a big sensation like this, all that mattered was which side you were on. Were you in a position where you could speak on the subject, or were you stuck groveling to others, begging for them to tell you more? Those were the only two possibilities. And now, all those gathered there were trying desperately to be on the side that could do the talking.

Basically, it went like this: someone had picked up a broken radio that he found by chance and fixed it. But, unable to receive any kind of signal, white noise was all that was coming through. He had tried everything from adjusting the needle to stretching out the antenna, but all of it was to no avail. Finally he gave up and, just as he was about to cut the power...

He heard it.

A "very beautiful voice" from nowhere. And he didn't just hear it. It was asking him, the owner of the radio, a question.

That is to say, it was speaking to him.

From some faraway land, someone was speaking to him through this discarded radio in this particular spot in Japan that was quite possibly the epitome of the word "boondocks." That alone was enough to make it a so-called "hot topic," but the question itself was of utmost significance as well. That was, after all, likely to be the main focus of people's chatter. What's more, it was a question that he couldn't immediately answer. That was enough to make the subject all the more interesting.

In the end, the owner of the radio called his friend over. They listened to the voice again together. When the friend was just as unable to come up with a response, they called over yet another friend. By then, the voice had gone silent. However, at the same time the next day, it returned. More friends were called over. Finally, "today" came. It was the day on which we would all listen to the voice together and decide whether or not to answer. The owner of the radio almost seemed afraid. The others who had heard the voice by now refused to utter the question aloud.

What would happen if we answered? That was the fear spurring our exhilaration.

"What if it's not a human?" one kid said.

"KRRSSSSHSSHHHHZHRR," said another, trying to curb his nervousness by imitating the sound of the white noise.

"I'm...going home," yet another kid said, only to be instantly pulled back in by everyone else. I might've even been that coward. I seem to have some nebulous memory of someone saying, "No way, Kazuki. We'll all listen together." It's hard to remember, but it probably was me. Even looking at how I am now, I think so.

Being in that place at that time meant being in the very center of what would undoubtedly become the talk of the town. Regardless of whether or not we would actually get to hear the voice. Maybe it was our mission to be there; maybe it was our test.

That old silver radio, with its cord wrapped around a branch of the camphor tree. The antenna extending from the tip of the branch, desperately reaching toward the heavens. The three friends acting as one to assign the lot of us the mission of listening to the droning white noise with a pricked ear.

Thinking about it now, it really makes for a charming image. The innocent actions of those who knew nothing.

Or maybe *actions* is too strong a word. These were only hopes.

But no one would have ever believed these hopes would really invite something.

In an instant, the charm of the situation did an about-face.

The white noise crackled, then disappeared, leaving a ringing in our ears. The radio became perfectly silent, and we all held our breaths. It was as though all sound had been sucked out of the world.

A voice came through, painfully clear, as if gently stroking our very hearts.

"Are you—KRRSSHHZZZSSHRR—"

Chapter One
Into The Unseen World

Chapter One
Into The Unseen World

"**R**emember!"

Fierce encouragement traveled directly from the Siegfried System to the brain. It wasn't directed to an individual unit, but rather a simultaneous transmission dispatched to all units currently engaged in battle.

Kazuki charged his Mark Elf as he felt the transmission go straight into his mind without bothering to pass through his ears. The jet-black machine, now transformed into a giant mass of fighting spirit, dashed forth.

"You are all pilots who have undergone one hundred-fifty credits of hypnotic training. As long as you stick tight to the optimum combat pattern drawn from the R-complex, this'll be a walk in the park." Words from the System these pilots had heard a million times, sent to arouse the fighting spirit.

The R-complex—also known as the Reptilian complex. The core of the human mind. The part which governs our most fundamental instincts and the source of all hostility and bloodlust.

The pilots' number one goal lay in accepting full activation of the R-complex during battle. Developed through hypnotic learning and repeated intensive training, the R-complex would bring forth all of the pilots' aggression and thirst for violence. Consequently, all of these welled up impulses would transform into a desire to link with the physical sensory area found in the cerebellum.

In other words, in order to fill their heads with a desire to destroy their opponents, in order to *actually* destroy their opponents, the pilots had to concentrate with all their might on moving their arms and legs, on honing their five senses.

After that, the optimum attack pattern in a list of some ten million buried deep within their subconscious minds would automatically surface, and the machine would move thus.

Kazuki's Mark Elf advanced approximately fifty meters, built up some pressure in the knees, and then released it all in an instant, leaping into the air. The jet-black machine soared upward, a 1.5-ton super-conductive assault rifle resting in its arms, and landed on a rocky stretch more than ten meters above. A cloud of dust rose up with a thunderous roar, the individual grains brushing against the surface of the great war machine and sending reverse feedback to Kazuki's skin sensors. It felt like he was really in the midst of a dust cloud himself.

He could feel the trigger of his rifle clearly by its chill.

I am the Mark Elf.

Strong thoughts urged on his unification with the machine.

The Mark Elf is me.

And then, he ran. It was the kind of all-out sprint that pushed the capabilities of the machine's limbs and skeleton—both forged of a refined mix of ultra-hard alloyed frames and soft, flexible steel—to the limit.

"Confirm positions and distances of all units. Odd numbers forward. Even numbers disperse." As the voice from the System gave its orders, a specific route tracing number of enemies, enemy types, confirmed enemy attack patterns, and unit correspondence criteria raced through Kazuki's mind.

The sensation excited Kazuki so much that he wanted to shout at the top of his lungs. It was a perfectly natural response. It was proof that he was totally unified with the machine and with this System. Without actually yelling, he ground his molars instead. He felt his temples throbbing.

The enemy was dead ahead. The nine units currently enabled for combat headed for the enemy units in the rear as ordered by the System.

The battlefield was a small island off the southwest coast of the main island. It was an artificial territory created specifically for the purpose of engaging the enemy. In times of battle, a reactor on the main island would release energy, creating an invisible defense barrier comprised of two concentric circles. The current battlefield was locked between those two circles in a region known as the War Zone.

Frantically, they had chased the enemy here. As long as they were inside the War Zone, the chances of the main island taking damage dropped significantly, even if it became a fierce-fought battle.

Right now, they and the enemy were the only ones here. Even if they were to beg and scream to be let out, the adults back on the island would never do something as stupid as lower the defense shields. Even if their own child was the one doing the begging and screaming.

It was that very fear that obliterated any sense of awkwardness in unifying oneself with the machine. These ridiculously long arms don't belong to me, you might say. My joints don't work like this, you might say. I'm not this gigantic, you might say. But even a small hint of such awkwardness would spell a late arrival to the fight, your defeat at the hands of the enemy, and your inability to go home.

The important thing was acceptance. Acceptance of the situation. Of the current self. Of this jet-black machine, created in the image of man, but somehow evoking the image of a reptile. The key was in believing all of these things were your own. If you couldn't do that, you quite literally wouldn't even be able to open the machine's eyes. By now, Kazuki had seen a great number of pilot candidates who ended up curled in little fetal balls, their eyes shut tight the instant they entered their unit.

But he was different. From the very first time he had entered his unit, he had been able to endure these sensations of discomfort and eventually accept them. Now, he was even able to control the machine's eyesight with complete freedom. The machine's field of vision gave a "goat's eye view," stretching around two hundred-eighty degrees. But so what if he could see over his own shoulder when he was looking straight ahead?

As Kazuki ran forth, he zoomed in on a particular area of that goat's eye view, activating the "eagle eye view" that was capable of seeing objects two hundred kilometers away. It was as though a telescope had emerged in the center of his vision.

Engaged in close quarters combat approximately a kilometer away, the Mark Ein and Mark Drei leapt into his vision. At the same time, he confirmed the presence of something truly beautiful.

The head and arms closely resembled those of a human, but its similarity to a man ended there. The face was somehow suggestive of some kind of foreign mask, but it couldn't be said for sure whether it really was a face. It could've been just another tentacle.

It was slightly larger than Kazuki's own unit, roughly the size of a thirteen-story building. In spite of its enormous mass, however, it had nothing that could be identified as legs, and instead floated silently above the ground.

From back to front it was covered in crystal, and the whole thing sparkled gold. It was enough to take one's breath away. If you approached even closer, you would likely be able to see rainbow-colored sparkles within the gold. It was as though all the jewels in the world had been gathered together, given life, and emitted a bright light in exchange.

Its beauty was enough to make you wonder if God Himself had descended from the heavens the first time you laid eyes on it. The more you gazed into its reflection, the more it would suck you in. Kazuki—the

Mark Elf—aimed his rifle at it.

He dashed forth with a fiery readiness for combat as the current status of Mark Ein and Mark Drei was sent directly from the System to his brain.

There was no real problem with Mark Ein. Its right arm and leg had been mangled by the enemy, spraying shock-absorbing stratified liquid mercury everywhere like blue blood, but that was the extent of it. It had also apparently taken chest damage, and the Mark Ein's ash-colored torso frame was covered in the same blue blood. But as the damage had failed to penetrate the cockpit, the "pain" accompanying the collision had failed to cause heart paralysis. The pilot was still very much alive.

The problem was with Mark Drei.

The enemy's arms were wrapped around the unit like tentacles, several times over. The sparkling golden enemy eroded through the yellow rose-colored unit at an alarming rate. The person ensnared by this abominable jewel would soon become one of them.

The enemy's most fearsome high-level attack: Assimilation.

Using its remaining left arm, the Mark Ein desperately pummeled away at the enemy with the blade of its Ruga Lance in an attempt to free the captured target of this deadly phenomenon. If well executed, there was a chance of cutting the Mark Drei away from the enemy to rescue the pilot within. But the attempt proved a spectacular failure. Mark Ein's lance was caught between the teeth of a second face which emerged from the enemy's back—it was caught by a tentacle disguised as a human face—and its trajectory was deflected. The blade emitted an intense heat as it met a fruitless collision with the ground. In the same moment—

Mark Drei again?

The thought crossed Kazuki's mind.

The notorious Mark Drei was also known as the "Yellow Coffin." It was the unit that had sent seven different pilots to that true land of peace somewhere far up in the sky. Of course, it was just a coincidence; nothing more than a jinx. Similarly, it was only a coincidence that the odd numbered units, whose main priority was close combat, took more damage. Enemies came from every direction in all manner of forms. Everyone had an equal chance to be sent to Heaven. But Mark Drei had somehow overcome these equal odds to become the one unit that was always jinxed. The scene unfolding before Kazuki's eyes was eloquently telling of that.

Long before Kazuki hesitated, the Mark Ein had already taken the appropriate action.

It pulled the trigger of its rifle. A stream of fire shot at the enemy assimilating with Mark Drei. The bullet, leaving a trail of blue flame as it traveled at supersonic speed, shot through the enemy's tentacle arm, blasting away the Mark Drei's chest. But the Mark Drei remained in the enemy's grasp. It became apparent that the enemy's tentacles had dug all the way into the torso.

Kazuki continued firing as he closed in on the enemy. He was probably screaming, but the sound of the gunfire muffled his own voice. The bullets had no shell casing, instead being propelled electrically. Each shot delivered the force of a missile. It was enough to shatter all the windows in a building if the gun was in close enough range when it was fired.

Taking in every single shot, the enemy still failed to even budge. It had raised a high-level protective barrier, so the trails of blue flame never even reached it. Though invisible to the naked eye, the barrier destroyed anything that touched it.

There was only one way to destroy this beautiful golden being protected by its force field. Kazuki would have to approach even closer, stepping into range for the enemy to assimilate him. Once that had been done, he could finally exploit the true power of his machine by entering the Assimilation mode. He would go through the enemy's barrier himself and allow the Assimilation to begin. This would allow him to come into direct contact—in other words, to exchange blows. Of course, it would have to be right before being assimilated. It was essentially a question of who would be able to get the first strike.

In an exhibition of its full potential, the Mark Elf charged head-first into the enemy's barrier and burst through. If it hadn't been in Assimilate Mode, the machine would have been crushed and mangled from the head down, and likely the cockpit would've suffered the same fate.

Instead, Kazuki plunged the barrel of his rifle as far into the enemy's chest as he could. *Into*. Ignoring the possibility of damaging the barrel, he jammed the entire shaft of the weapon into the enemy's body. Then, just like that, he fired.

The enemy's torso blew open. Most of the tentacle that had been wrapped around Mark Drei, as well as Mark Elf's rifle and the left arm supporting it, blew to smithereens with a burst of blue flame. At the same time, Kazuki was struck with the pain of his arm exploding from the elbow down. It only lasted a moment. The next instant, the left arm's Pain Block was activated by the System. The destroyed upper left arm's sensors cut off, and the pain vanished before the pilot lost consciousness.

By that point, the Mark Elf's remaining right arm was already gripping a new weapon. It was a weapon stored in the armor of the upper arm—a short sword-model mine. Kazuki swung it downwards, directly into the destroyed torso of the enemy. The blade plunged into the enemy's open wound and broke off. But that didn't mean the weapon was damaged. Just like a cutter blade, it only took a small application of pressure to the side for this blade to break.

The next instant, the blade exploded. It was a blade-shaped bomb. Normally, it would be set to explode two seconds after the blade snapped off, but Kazuki had reset it to 0.2 seconds.

The enemy's gorgeous golden torso blew inside out and burst into flames. Within the newly formed chesthole, an intense light shone out like a blast furnace. It was the enemy's true essence, an organic crystal heart known as the *core*. In actuality, the golden body was nothing more than a sort of armor. If you didn't destroy the enemy's true essence buried within, its vitality was infinite. In that sense, it was the same as the relationship between machine and pilot. You could always restore a machine, but once a pilot's life was extinguished it was all over. And Kazuki prayed that it would all be over as he plunged another blade deep into the beautiful, shining core.

At the same time, the enemy's tentacles lunged out at him. They pierced through the upper region of both legs and tore through his chest. An instant before his vision went pitch black from pain, he snapped the blade once again. As it exploded, the core blasted out of the enemy's chest cavity in bits. It was like a sparkling scarlet flood of jewels. With a beauty so captivating as to make you wonder if it was really from this universe, the enemy's body began to change.

It began changing from its sparkling golden state to a livid black. Drained of its power, the crystalline enemy crumbled into a pile of dried up dirt. As common an occurrence as it was, it was like something out of a fairytale. Kazuki felt like some foolish king, given a clump of dirt and convinced it was gold.

The feeling was immediately slapped away by a rousing voice.

"Mark Elf, enemy to the rear!"

Fully comprehending the meaning of these words, Kazuki whipped around. The countless number of tentacles that had been lodged in Mark Drei's belly lashed forth like whips. Kazuki promptly strafed to the side, but the writhing, blade-like tentacles managed to slice through his right leg all the way to the inner bone. His foot hung on by a thread. If he fell, he would be sliced to bits. Enduring the pain, he somehow miraculously managed to maintain balance in his machine. He produced another exploding blade.

The enemy was growing out of the Mark Drei's lower abdomen. It had assimilated the pilot within, turning him into a mere piece of core. Beneath Kazuki's blade was the most deplorable thing in the world—an assimilated ally. Someone Kazuki had probably spoken to himself, just before the sortie.

You couldn't think about it. You had to stick that blade in before you had a chance to remember their face or name. That was the right thing to do. Even taking a split second to remind yourself so would prove lethal.

Taking no time to think, Kazuki was just about to swing down his blade when...

He heard a voice.

"Are you—"

It was gentle, as if stroking his very heart.

It wasn't coming from the System.

Reacting to the Mark Elf's Assimilate Mode, the enemy was communicating directly with Kazuki's mind. It was possible that the enemy had stolen the assimilated pilot's memories and learned of Kazuki's existence. Something about the tone of the voice seemed to say, "I know all about you." It sent a chill up his spine.

But before the enemy could utter the entire question, it was obliterated. It was just before Kazuki had a chance to swing down his blade. The lower abdomen of the Mark Drei blew apart in an explosion of blue flame, right before Kazuki's eyes.

He heard gunfire from behind. Once again he

snapped out of the daze of trying to kill his own ally. Shaking the feeling away, he shifted his glance to the unit providing him backup.

A unit armed with a gigantic rifle approached from the right side. Kazuki stared at it, a bit stunned. The blue-gray unit—Mark Vier. It was one of the even-numbered units dispersed to confuse the enemy. Likely, it had come here to provide backup in compliance with the System's orders. And then, without even a second's hesitation, it had pulled the trigger and turned Mark Drei into a coffin for the eighth time.

The Mark Vier came to a halt and held up its weapon for show. It was a gesture meant to say, "Backup complete." Or, perhaps, "That's what I'm here for."

That's what I'm here for. If an ally gets assimilated, call on Mark Vier. It was a joke among the pilots that received no laughter.

"Koyo the Friend Killer." It was the nickname of the boy piloting Mark Vier. The other pilots first gave him the name after he killed three assimilated allies, but no one would dare say it to his face. There was something very sinister about the Friend Killer's demeanor, considering one's life might at some point depend on him, and all the other pilots secretly held him in great awe.

All, that is, except for Kazuki and one other.

In reality, it wasn't until after the nickname had stuck that Mark Vier's pilot had really overcome hesitation in killing his allies. It was a fact that only Kazuki and the controller of the System were aware of.

"Annihilation of enemy presence confirmed.

Lowering magnetic shield. All units, return to base. Retrieve all possible destroyed units. Pilots who have sustained heavy damage, blank your consciousness and prepare units for auto-flight."

Heavy damage, blah blah blah. Is that supposed to mean me? Kazuki wondered. Mark Vier paid no more attention to him and charged off to meet the other even-numbered units. At this point, the System began making individual transmissions rather than addressing the entire fleet.

"Kazuki, blank out. If I block any more of your pain sensors, your movement will become extremely sluggish."

"Hey, Soshi..." Kazuki said. He could tell how much damage he had taken by the intense pain caused just by trying to speak. A reply came right away. It was a reply from the one person Kazuki both trusted and doubted more than anyone in the whole world, the person in control of the System, the person who had them running around in the depths of Hell.

"What, Kazuki?"

"I want to ask a favor."

"A favor?"

"I can't remember who was piloting Mark Drei. Will you tell me?" Even Kazuki was aware that he was being frivolous when he ought to be making haste. But he just couldn't help asking.

He felt a sudden presence at his flank.

A red phantom appeared. A single boy. It was the mirror projection of Soshi, operator of the System. All pilots were in a state where they shared a portion of

Soshi's nervous system—a portion of his consciousness and emotions. Because of this, when he focused his consciousness on a given pilot, that pilot would be aware of his presence as if he were a reflection in a mirror. He was a phantom dyed in red, from the hair to the eyes to the cheeks.

The reason was simple. Because they shared a collective consciousness, it was just as if he was inside Kazuki. If you asked a person what the inside of their body looked like, not many people would think of blue or yellow. Most people would think red—the color of blood. Particularly in Kazuki's case, Soshi appeared as a transparent red image.

"There were two deaths in this battle."

"You mean there was another one?"

"Both will be announced after you've returned to base. You should check at the next briefing after you've rested." It was his usual matter-of-fact way of speaking. He wore a cold expression that showed his utter lack of guilt or reserve, even when two friends had just died. That was Soshi's role. If the operator of the System exposed his own emotions, it would affect every single pilot. Thus, in order to take charge of the Siegfried System, a person had to be in control of his or her own emotions.

Soshi shared every pilot's pain and fear. This job demanded the willpower to suppress every single ounce of fear and pain felt by as many as twelve people. This was a fact Kazuki had learned at the start of the war. If Soshi seemed cold-blooded, it was all for the sake of the pilots.

"I want to know now," Kazuki said. A glint of something resembling pity flickered in Soshi's eye. Likewise, Kazuki half-shared his emotions. Soshi at the System helm knew how he felt.

We're just disposable goods, we're just batteries to make these machines run, and there are any number of replacements standing by, and I know exactly how I'll be disposed of if I die, but really I'm not at all ready to die and the very thought of death right now is making me nauseous. The same things Kazuki felt after every battle.

"If I confirm, you'll blank out immediately. Deal?"

"I promise," he murmured. Ever so faintly, a gentle smile seemed to appear on Soshi's face. An instant before Soshi's phantom disappeared, Kazuki's awareness shifted to his left eye. To the single line of a scar carved into Soshi's face, from the top of his eyelid down the cheek—the scar that robbed his left eye of light. Before Kazuki's emotions towards the scar could swell up, Soshi vanished. In his place, the war casualty data began to race through Kazuki's head. If he focused his consciousness, he could toggle it on and off via an imaginary monitor produced before his eyes. But without bothering to do so, he simply absorbed the muddled stream of information coming in.

In addition to Mark Drei, the pilot of Mark Acht had also perished. Even among the other even-numbered units, whose primary forms of action lay in guerilla and disturbance tactics, the Mark Acht had been designed to exhibit superior prowess in engaging enemies on the front line. Whether the pilot's death had been caused by his inability to harness that power, some fatal mistake, or a newly generated enemy attack pattern—that was for the adults to figure out.

At last, he would know who it was—who had died. He knew it wouldn't be any comfort. Still, at least he could spend his last few moments before blanking out confessing his honest feelings that he was glad it was he who had died.

Dragged along by the pain and a suddenly drained spirit, he realized in a daze that he was staring up at the sky. He was searching for someone good at supplying aerial support. He was searching for a unit as pure white as a swan—the Mark Sechs. But its existence had been blanked out. No one ever spoke of the Sixth Unit anymore. Mark Sechs wasn't there. It was eternally blanked.

He recalled this and, before letting it get him too depressed, switched his consciousness to blank out.

His consciousness completely extinguished, the machine switched to auto-flight mode as he slept. Quick movement was impossible in this state, but he didn't have anyone to go rescue, so, as long as he got back to base, there wouldn't be any problem. But most importantly, these were Soshi's orders and concerns, so what did it matter if he wanted to escape the pain and anguish? Such were Kazuki's excuses.

There was an unpleasant feeling like "death" when you blanked out. However, Kazuki hastily dove into the sensation as if trying to escape. His vision went dark and the tragic sight of the destroyed "Yellow

Coffin" faded away. Likewise vanished the names of the two deceased he had only just now checked, as did his thoughts about Koyo the Friend Killer. As did his thoughts about the Eternal Blank. As did Soshi's scar. Everything disappeared, and, at last, Kazuki remembered Peace. Himself before the war. His feelings before the world became a piece of a bigger puzzle.

The battle now over, the Mark Elf dragged its shredded leg along as it carried him like a child in a cradle. It was a cradle of warmth and safety, free of any and all peril, almost eerily absent of anything that might arouse a will to fight or ignite one's ferocity. And deep within that cradle, well—Kazuki was there.

The old Kazuki, the one who knew nothing, who was living out an existence that took Peace for granted—he was there.

He dreamed.

In the midst of darkness so black he couldn't even see his own hands, all he could hear were the echoes of crashing waves. In the sea on a dark night, Kazuki swam alone. As hard and desperately as he swam, his arms and legs only grew numb more quickly. It was that kind of chilling ocean.

Before long, the energy was gone from his body and he seemed destined to fall victim to the pitch black ocean, which would swallow him into its depths.

Then, as if to rescue him from that fear, a faint light appeared in the distance. And Kazuki knew. He had swum this far towards that light. He pushed his remaining strength into his numb and frozen arms and legs, waves beating against his cheeks, and swam. Slowly, the light that had saved him from a watery death drew closer and closer. His heart was filled to the brim with gratitude for the light, simply for being there, as well as with a desire to escape.

And so he reached the shore. He clung to a steep rock and crawled his way up to the top, where he heard echoes of warm laughter. He raised his head to discover that the light was emanating from a large shelter, and he could see it bustling with life through each window. There were friends together laughing. There were families enjoying one another's company. People who appeared to be lovers. But all of them were vague, elusive silhouettes.

Kazuki wondered if his light was somewhere among these rows of windows, and he scanned them over.

"I can't do that..." he felt, no matter which window he looked into. He couldn't go inside. This window, that window—there was no place for him.

He continued staring into the lights for a while, but eventually he let go of the rock and let the waves pull him back in. Before he knew it, the lights were behind him and he was swimming again. The lights grew distant, and he once again found himself in the midst of the pitch black ocean, squeezing drops of strength into his numb arms and legs.

Kazuki kicked away his blankets with a start.

"Huh?"

Man, it's cold, the thought blinked on and off somewhere inside his sleep-addled brain.

Oh, it's the ocean.

He was nearly convinced until he looked up to discover the ceiling of the old tatami room in the pale, early morning light. *Oh wait. This is my room, not the ocean,* he realized. *That's right. It's just cold because it's April. Hey, school starts back up today.*

But hey, April is spring. Shouldn't it be warmer? Now his mind had a counter-argument going. *Hmm, but early spring mornings do still get pretty chilly. 'Specially if you don't have any blankets. Speaking of which, shouldn't I have blankets? We're not that poor,* he thought, and then groped around until he found them and pulled them back over himself. Wrapped at last in the warmth of his blankets, he recalled that he had been dreaming.

Ah, that dream, he thought. It wasn't that he had the same dream every single night, but it was recurring. Swimming desperately in the middle of a dark ocean, until he came across a remarkably lively house—only to be scared away. The minute details seemed to change each time, but the dream was essentially the same.

It was such a terribly cold ocean. Even after waking up, even now, he could vividly recall that icy numbness in his arms and legs. It was a mystery to him how he was able to have such lifelike dreams of the freezing cold, all while wrapped up in these warm blankets. He wondered if it was because of yesterday's game of "Icy Ocean Baseball." In fact, that was obviously the reason.

Tatsumiya Island was impressive in name only, and the reality was that it was an island in the middle of nowhere, covered in mountains and surrounded by ocean, and almost completely bare of amusements of any kind. Radio waves couldn't reach it and they only received local television channels. Newspapers arrived four days late, magazines two weeks. If all of Japan was obliterated in a mega-earthquake, foreign countries would've gotten the news before them. It was an isolated island, both physically and culturally. But the young boys of the island made the most of their situation, exploiting their overabundant vitality and relatively feeble power of invention in order to have fun. Yesterday's game of Ocean Baseball—the icy version, no less—was really nothing more than a pointless test of one's limits. The game itself, which originated from a debate over how to play baseball on an island with so little flat land, was essentially a glorified version of baseball that took place straddling the line between land and sea.

Home base was on the beach, while second base was a red rubber buoy floating in the water. The red indicated that the water was three meters deep at that spot. For first and third base, the small group of boys who had originally come up with the idea for Ocean Baseball had taken wooden stakes nearly a meter long and spent four days hammering them into the ground, right on the water's edge. After that, they topped the stakes with rubber plates to keep them firmly set. But the shoreline was a trickster, and the next thing they knew, the tide had risen and the bases were in the middle of the sea. Because of how extremely detrimental the water was to a runner's movements, this game demanded a fisherman-like attention to wind direction, the ebb and flow of the tides, and even the timing with which offense and defense rotated.

The factor of regionality was what ignited the children's passion for this game. Built between two steep inclines, the town's eastern and western sides were known, respectively, as the "Eastern Slope" and "Western Slope." Every little thing was a competition based on which side you belonged to. Western Slope is close to the candy store, so it's more convenient. But the Eastern Slope has the bathhouse, so it's the best. The Western Slope is right by the school and hospital. The Eastern Slope is right by the fish store, liquor store, and shrine, so it's easy to throw festivals.

And thus, over the past two years, the sport of Ocean Baseball had fast become the one and only official settling ground for disputes between the two sides, with parents even showing up to watch games sometimes.

Kazuki, who had come to be affiliated with the Western Slope, had also become something of a "secret weapon" for his team. He was never the type to stand out in his day-to-day life at school, but when it came to sports of any kind, he would crush the opposition so soundly that it was almost as if he were cheating. Even among the other junior high students who prided themselves on their physical strength, he seemed to be the most athletically gifted by a long shot.

"Seemed," that is, because Kazuki himself had no such self image. He didn't think something like beating the second place runner in a marathon by a difference of a whole minute was anything particular to brag about, and grabbing first place in short, medium, and long-distance races was just an everyday occurrence for him. He was victim to that misguided logic often found in people blessed with exceptional talent.

Why doesn't everybody try harder? he would think. *If they took this more seriously, so would I.*

When spring break came, they couldn't just let their magnificent "secret weapon" go off and enjoy himself. That was the thinking of his Western Slope Ocean Baseball teammates.

"Eh, I'm not so great at baseball," Kazuki would always reply. But for someone who boasted such absolute, unrivaled skill in both offense and defense, had an 80% batting average, could run the fifty-meter dash in five seconds, and held the school record for distance throws, such a statement was unforgivable. "You're a member of the Western Slope, too," they would say, suppressing his protests with totalitarian force and dragging him onto the playing field. In turn, the Eastern Slope team's desire to win would ignite full force as they bemoaned the presence of Kazuki on the opposing team, and a fierce game would commence in the midst of the chill of the blowing wind, in temperatures that never rose above ten degrees Celsius even in the middle of the day.

"I must've swum about twenty kilometers," Kazuki recalled with a mind still half-asleep.

The surefire way to win Ocean Baseball was to hit longball after longball. If you hit the ball out to sea, the defending team would have to swim like mad to retrieve it. It was common for the tides to turn a pop fly into a home run. But when Kazuki was in the outfield, he would calmly, naturally swim out and retrieve the ball, bringing all of the Eastern Slope team's hits to naught. When he was up to bat, on the other hand, without fail someone would yell, "Get an extra ball ready!" On that particular day, they had lost three balls thanks to Kazuki. Not to mention the fact that it was a soft ball and a plastic bat. He was monstrous.

Despite this, Kazuki was very thin. He wasn't at all what you would call "bulky." In reality, this was because he only had as much muscle as he needed to use without stunting his flexibility, but at first glance, the sight of this skinny-framed boy smashing balls out to sea was beyond "cool," instead filling all players on both teams with a sense of horror.

"Don't use Kazuki, or all the balls will disappear," the Eastern Slope kids would rationally complain. Even the Western Slope kids occasionally wondered, in all seriousness, "Isn't it kind of cowardly to use him?" It seemed like a terrible comment to make about one's own teammate, but that was how much he stood out. It was simply a fact.

Kazuki just did as he was told. Nothing more, nothing less. As a result, he had no say in whether they would view him as an asset or just alienate him. Alternatively, if everyone just lost themselves in the game, he just had to go along with it.

That was how he really felt, this boy called Kazuki.

The image of those windows, casting light into the black ocean, popped into his mind once again. Just then, his alarm went off.

After changing clothes, Kazuki left his room and went downstairs. His father, Fumihiko, was already awake and kneading clay. He had probably been out at oh-dark-thirty fetching it from the hills out back. And now he was mixing it together with a meticulousness incomprehensible to Kazuki.

The first floor of the house was covered in dishware as far as the eye could see. The myriad ceramic pots and bowls crammed into wooden shelves were all the work of his father. They were his merchandise. An old, wooden sign with the words "Makabe Dishware" on it hung in front of their house.

"You're up," Fumihiko said without looking up from his clay.

"Yeah."

Conversation over. That was generally how they went.

Kazuki passed through the living room that separated the work area from the shop, and whipped up a quick breakfast. Going through habitualized motions he could've done in his sleep at this point, he put together some rice, miso soup, and a few other small dishes and set two places in the living room.

As he did this, Fumihiko came in to join him.

"Thanks."

"Sure."

Conversation complete. Commence sitting. Begin the meal.

And so they dimly greeted another ordinary day. With nothing in particular to say, they ate in silence. They ate with his father's leftover hand-made merchandise. For as long as Kazuki could remember, there was an unspoken understanding between the two of them: Dad made the dishes, and he made what went in them. It had always been his job to prepare the food.

What he had *never* understood, however, was the bowl he was currently holding in his hand. *Was* it a bowl? The shape of it was enough to raise doubts. It was distorted in a dramatic, even explosive, kind of way. It was so poorly balanced in form that it seemed a miracle that it didn't fall over when you put it on a flat surface. He almost wondered if his father had gotten sick of making it when it was only halfway finished and just smooshed the whole thing in his hand. But with so many of the dishes lined up around the store so closely resembling this one, he was convinced this was just his father Fumihiko's art style.

Sometimes he truly wondered how they sold at all. If they didn't sell, the two of them wouldn't be able to maintain such a lifestyle. The fact that his father was actually able to provide him with food seemed to Kazuki to be one of the Seven Wonders of the World.

Every once in a while, Kazuki would find himself in a scene where all the adults of the island referred to his father as "Mr. Artist." He assumed it was their euphemism for "the weirdo."

Then again, sometimes he'd take a look at his

father and see that there really was something artistic about him. Unlike his style of pottery, there was always a sense of quiet dignity about the man himself. He rarely smiled, but he never seemed particularly angry, either. It was like he had the word "calm" written on his face. Physically, he closely resembled Kazuki in that he appeared very slender, but it was only because he was so tall. Possibly because he was always duking it out with his clay, his body was, in reality, as solid as a stump. Kazuki supposed there was something artistic about his father's aloofness.

"So today's a new semester?" Fumihiko asked as their meal was coming to an end.

"Hm?" Kazuki said quizzically as he stacked his empty dishes.

"Be sure to say something to your mother."

"Right."

That's what you wanted to say? Kazuki wondered, somehow not immediately satisfied. It seemed like the kind of thing that didn't need to be said, and, indeed, Fumihiko had probably only said it to be sure.

Kazuki set the dishes in the kitchen. Washing them was Fumihiko's job. Occasionally, he would neglect to do so and Kazuki would end up washing them, but, at any rate, he could leave it to his father for now.

"See you later," he said after preparing for school, as Fumihiko stacked his dishes.

"Yep." Kazuki received the short response with his back and exited through the dish-adorned front of the store. On his way, he took a glance over at one specific shelf. On it was a plain picture stand with a picture of a woman holding a young child. It was his mother, smiling as she held a young Kazuki. This photograph was all he knew of her. He was so young when she died that he didn't even remember her voice.

With no Buddhist altar in the house, he faced the photograph instead. *I'll see you later,* he said silently before he left the house.

One step out the door led to a stone staircase running from right to left. It was the kind of steep staircase that most people would be eager to avoid, but Kazuki quickly made his way up the stairs without giving it a second thought. He came to a tranquil path and began heading in the direction of the school when someone called out to him from a side street.

"Just in time!"

Whoever it was sounded truly happy. The voice was followed by the dry sound of spinning bicycle tires. It was a girl, for some reason pushing her bike instead of riding it.

"G'morning, Kazuki-kun. You were in yesterday's baseball game, right? My sister went and watched. She was cheering about how the Western Slope won again."

"Oh, yeah." Kazuki was always troubled at times like this. Possibly because he lived with just his father, whenever someone confronted him with a barrage of topics like this he would find himself at a loss for a response. Not to mention that this was the first time he'd seen this girl since before spring break. It was the best he could do to mutter something back.

"Good morning, Tomi." Might as well start with a greeting. She had said his name, so he did likewise. Next was the topic of baseball. More important than whether or not he had participated, the Western Slope had indeed won, so he thought it best to confirm that fact. But how to phrase it?

"Hey, don't be so perplexed." Her voice, somehow sweet to the ear, interrupted his thought process. It wasn't that she had *sweetened* her voice. There was something naturally sweet about it. It was the kind of voice you never wanted to stop listening to.

"Huh?" A few beats later he came back to his senses. Did she just call him perplexed?

But she giggled at him and said, "Sorry, I've been doing all the talking. Maybe I'm just excited because it's the start of a new semester. I haven't seen you in awhile, and all. Funny how I'm the type whose natural reaction is to talk and you're the type whose natural reaction is to clam up, huh?"

It was like his mind and personality were completely transparent to her. Reflexively, Kazuki tried to retort, but gave up before the words came out. The girl before him right now was none other than Maya Tomi.

One of the many things people from the Western Slope liked to brag about was that they lived near the hospital. It was the Tomi Hospital, to be precise, and Maya was the Tomis' daughter. She came from a family of doctors, her mother being a physician and her older sister being a public health doctor at a school. Her dad wasn't around, apparently because her parents had divorced when she was still young. In many ways, she was the exact opposite of Kazuki.

There was nothing you could hide from this girl. Perhaps she had inherited some amazing super-ability from her parents, because she had a catch phrase: "I think I get it."

Example number one:

Someone broke one of the windows in the school. Nobody knew who the culprit was. The next day, a boy passed by Maya in the hall. "G'morning," she said. "Good thing you didn't cut your hand on that glass, huh?" The boy, who was in fact the culprit, went straight to the office and confessed. He thought Maya had seen him. But she hadn't.

Example number two:

A certain girl got into a fight with her mother, and then went off to school feeling rather gloomy. Instead of letting her feelings show, she just smiled cheerfully and joked around. "Hey. Apologize to your mom," was all Maya had to say. They say after that day, the girl was too afraid to ever speak to Maya again.

Example number three:

On his way to greet the starting semester of his third year of junior high school, Makabe Kazuki had run into Maya, who called out to him, and he was perplexed as to how to respond. "Don't be so perplexed," she laughed.

So that was what she was all about.

Kazuki lived particularly close to Maya, and they left for school at roughly the same time. Moreover,

her mother's hospital was where he would go when he
was sick, and even when they were kids he often ate
dinner at the Tomi residence and got her mother and
sister to teach him how to cook.

As a result, he had interacted with Tomi many
times. Once, regarding her seemingly supernatural
ability to read people's minds, he had asked her, "Can
you tell what I'm thinking right now?" He had spoken
with a grave seriousness.

"Yeah, as if. You're so weird, Kazuki-kun." Her
smile was clear as sunshine. "But sometimes you just
know what people are keeping bottled up inside, just
by some little gesture or glance or twitch of the mouth,
right?" she had said.

For example, a boy who broke a window
might wear a slightly unusual expression whenever he
looked at a window or he might try to hide his hand,
or something. A girl who fought with her mom might
glance at the floor every time something that reminded
her of her mother came up in conversation, or she might
bow her head just a bit as if apologizing.

"Everyone does stuff like that, right?" Maya
said.

So that's it, Kazuki thought, convinced. But
he couldn't help but wonder how common it was for
someone to even take note of such extremely subtle
gestures, much less possess the ability to analyze their
exact meaning.

Be that as it may, as the only son in a family
where parent and child alike were poor speakers, there
was nobody easier for Kazuki to talk to than Maya.

There were those who feared talking to her, but he wasn't one of them. With Maya, he could easily talk about anything.

Yes, anything.

Even the things he had kept hidden away in his heart, the anguish he shared with no one else. One time he had completely spilled the beans, answering any inquiry she presented in that strangely sweet voice. She still hadn't told anyone what he had said that day.

Maya walked alongside Kazuki without mounting her bicycle as its tires squeaked around and around.

"You know, Kazuki-kun, I was wondering if you'd be leaving around this time, and here you are," she smiled.

"Guess I'm easy to figure out, huh?"

"Well, I wouldn't say that. I just had a feeling. Even though it's a new semester, I just figured you'd go to school feeling the same way as always."

"Hm..."

She was right. School days and holidays never made much difference to Kazuki. They weren't the kind of thing that excited his emotions.

"Whenever a new semester begins, I always remember my first day of school. When I was six. First grade. It felt like everything in the world was about to change. I thought that if I looked in the mirror I'd see someone completely different than the person I had been up until then. I woke up bright and early in the morning just to look in the mirror, but it was just the usual reflection. I was a little disappointed, but pretty relieved, too."

A slight grin formed on Kazuki's face.

"As many times as I hear that story, it always seems so perfectly you."

"Huh? I tell this story a lot?" She wore a look of bewilderment. Kazuki couldn't help but snicker. During spring break, he had laughed out loud so few times he could've counted them.

"Three times a year."

"Three?"

"The first day after spring break, summer break, and winter break."

"Wha..." She blushed. Kazuki was the one reading her mind, for a change.

"Tomi, did you look in the mirror this morning, by any chance?"

"...Yes."

"Do you look in the mirror every time a new semester starts, by any chance?"

"Eheheh. Kinda. It's a habit, I guess."

"Do you want to become a new person?"

"I don't think that's it. I mean, I was really relieved today and stuff."

"Relieved?"

"Just one more year, right?"

"Ah..."

One more year. After that, neither of them would be junior high school students. On Tatsumiya Island, schooling ended with junior high. Once you had graduated, you basically had to either go find a job or leave the island to attend high school. Either way, you ended up leaving the island. Because of this, the population of the island consisted only of children in junior high school or below and their parents. Most of the middle generation lived in the satellite islands surrounding Tatsumiya. Collectively known as the "Adult Islands," they contained fishing grounds and factories, and were where people went to work when they became adults.

"Kazuki-kun...What're you going to do when the year is up?"

He hesitated for a moment, but it was meaningless to try and hide anything from her, so he answered. "I'm gonna go somewhere where nobody knows me."

He was not wishing, but affirming. It didn't matter where.

Work, high school, anything was fine. He knew it wouldn't be that easy to just go live on his own. But a strong feeling told him that he had to.

Perhaps he was thinking of a dark ocean visited by a row of windows. Of himself trying to get away...

"So you really are," Maya said after a moment's silence. "Will you come and visit the island sometimes?"

"I don't know...How about you? Gonna become a doctor?"

"Hm, I wonder. Mom and sis are doctors, so I could, but...I wonder. I don't know. But I like this island. Even if I go off and study or work somewhere, I'm sure I'll come back to visit."

"Huh."

"Come back and visit sometimes."

"Well, you never know what's ahead of you and all, so..."

"That doesn't matter. Just come back, because I'll probably always be here."

Kazuki sensed that Maya was feeling uneasy about something. But what? The fact that the world changes? The idea of becoming someone else? For Kazuki, those were both things he felt like he desired. It was probably Kazuki himself that was upsetting her. His ability to completely dismiss his life on this island.

"If I miss this place, I'll come back. Once in a while," he said. He hadn't even left, yet.

"Good," she laughed in that somehow sweet voice. She wore a true expression of happiness in light of Kazuki's words.

In the meantime, they had proceeded up a hill path and arrived in front of a house. Unusual for this particular island, it was a completely Western-style house. In the second story window, they could see a girl who wore a shy expression, as if she were surprised they had shown up.

"Shoko's wearing her uniform?" Maya said a bit glumly. She leaned her bicycle against the side of the house and looked back at Kazuki. "I'm going to talk to her for a bit before I go to school."

Kazuki nodded. Suddenly the bicycle made sense. It was for Shoko. On days when Shoko could go to school, Maya gave her a ride on her bike and they would go together. On days when she couldn't go to school, Maya would stay with her as long as she could and then rush to school on her bike alone.

Shoko. She was a regular at the Tomi Hospital. The frailest girl in all of Tatsumiya Island. On days when her anemia was particularly bad, just walking up a slope was enough to make her collapse. She carried a burden unfathomable to Kazuki, who could do two hundred times that much exercise without even breaking a sweat.

As a result, she was rarely able to attend school, but "Shoko Hazama" was a name most students in Kazuki's grade knew.

Whenever test scores were announced, she was, without fail, the highest. And it wasn't just in one subject. She was the top in every subject but physical education, in spite of the fact that she could barely even attend class. Or perhaps it was *because* she couldn't attend class and had to study like mad to make up for it.

"Shoko just doesn't want to be forgotten," Maya had once told Kazuki. Shoko wanted people to remember her, even if it was just by name. If Maya said it, that had to be the case. He had once asked her exactly what was wrong with Shoko. "Her liver," she had replied simply. Her tone of voice alone made it clear that it was an illness that couldn't easily be cured.

Shoko looked out at them from her windowsill with a slightly troubled expression and Kazuki stared blankly back.

"Wave to her," Maya said quietly. Both Kazuki and Shoko avoided eye contact.

"Huh?" Kazuki was about to reply, but was interrupted.

"Come on," Maya urged. He promptly waved a

hand at Shoko.

Shoko immediately disappeared, hiding herself from the window before Kazuki could blink.

"She went in. I guess she doesn't like me," Kazuki said, sounding not completely unhurt.

"That's not it," Maya grimaced. This time there was a slight taste of bitterness in that sweet voice of hers. "Well, I'm going to visit with Shoko for a while."

"Don't be late."

"I definitely won't. It would hurt Shoko," Maya said, pushing the classy-looking doorbell.

Kazuki, not having a bicycle, began to continue walking to school. Just then, he sensed someone's gaze. He looked up.

There, in the window, Shoko was looking his way and, ever so weakly, waving her hand. It seemed she didn't hate him after all.

Kazuki quickly waved back as if to say "Get better soon," then turned his back to her.

When he had almost arrived at school, Kazuki ran into someone else.

"Good morning, Kazuki." It was a gentle but carrying voice. Standing there was a friendly-looking boy wearing a bright smile.

"Good morning, Koyo," Kazuki said. Koyo gave him a pat on the shoulder.

"Good hustle yesterday."

"You were watching?"

"Just the last bit. You know, you ought to go

easy on them. Every time you got a hit, Tomi's sister would yell, 'It's outta here!'."

"They'll stop calling me to play sooner or later," Kazuki said readily. Koyo responded with a gentle shrug.

"They're not going to just let go of the Western Slope's secret weapon, you know. Good luck getting out." He wore what was the epitome of cheerful expressions, and his playful manner of speaking made you wonder if he was specially trained in cheering people up.

As with Maya, Koyo had been close friends with Kazuki since they were young. He was one of the precious few people Kazuki could comfortably talk to. His parents owned and operated the one and only Western-style café and restaurant on the whole island. Kazuki was a regular there. When he was a child, his lousy cook of a father would occasionally bring him there, and so he had grown close with Koyo.

Koyo was, in some ways, Kazuki's polar opposite. Amiable and eloquent, he was also extremely intellectual. When class grades were presented with boys and girls separated, Shoko Hazama and Koyo Kasugai would each take first place without exception.

And then there was his smile and words, both overflowing with sincerity. Indeed, the same was true of his heart.

This solid triumvirate of looks, brains, and heart allowed him to single-handedly monopolize popularity among the girls, whether they were younger, older, or of the same age, but he never took pride in it. At the same time, he was never aloof and always maintained a personable attitude with the utmost of delicacy.

His secret lay in his incredible memory, and it was something Kazuki could never hope to imitate.

"So when you were at bat near the end—"

Tomi's sister had a beer in her hand and yelled "Western Slope wins!!"

The old lady from Nishio's shop was nearby saying new balls were a hundred-twenty yen.

Kodate-san from the bathhouse was hollering about how members from both teams should come take a dip.

Koyo could regurgitate the motions and dialog of every single one of the twenty-six spectators there that day as if he were watching them right now.

That was Koyo.

"You remembered all that, huh?" Yesterday's events had already been swept off to some distant corner of Kazuki's memory. He was genuinely impressed. "I guess you never forget anything."

"That's not true," Koyo said as the school came into view over the hill.

"Come on. If you tell me that, I'll feel even worse about myself."

"There's one thing I can never remember no matter how hard I try. I think about it every time a new semester starts. You remember, right?"

"Huh?"

"Seven years ago, on March 31st, around 3:20 p.m.," Koyo prefaced with unsurpassable accuracy. "We were listening to that radio, remember?"

"Radio...?"

"The one picked up by the garbage dump."

"Oh..."

Kazuki seemed to recall something like that buried deep in his memory.

"They were talking about how you could hear a voice on the radio," Kōyo said, giving a specific roster of the three boys. They were all in the same grade as Kazuki. After the person who had picked it up did some tinkering around, the radio began emitting white noise, and supposedly they all heard a voice at some point.

"A voice? There was a voice?" Kazuki asked, feeling like it was finally starting to ring a bell.

"Yeah, I think so," Koyo replied in a way that was rather uncharacteristic. "Well, maybe I just thought there was a voice. You know, after just sitting there listening to white noise for all that time. Heh, it's kind of like my life right now," he said. It sounded like he was making some kind of quiet confession. The last thing he said made Kazuki remember something else. About Koyo's parents.

He couldn't remember when it was, exactly, but he had once gone to Koyo's family's restaurant with his father. Just as they were trying to leave, Koyo had said something to Kazuki in that same quiet, confessional tone.

"It must be nice to be able to have lunch with your dad, Kazuki."

Maybe, I guess, were Kazuki's only thoughts at the time. He didn't really grasp just how enviable this was to Koyo. It wasn't until much later that he learned how rarely Koyo ate meals with his parents. Most of the time, they just left some food prepared for him while they were either out working at the restaurant or drinking together without him.

Come to think of it, Kazuki recalled...

Back in elementary school, there had been a one-month period during which Koyo showed up in the exact same clothes every day, to the point that he got in trouble with the school. Supposedly, even then his parents hardly paid any attention to the situation. It sounded like a made-up story, but it was true. Koyo had told Kazuki about it, once. The clothes had been a birthday present from his parents. Of course, it wasn't really much of a celebration; just some leftover cake from the restaurant and a T-shirt they had picked out randomly and handed over to him, saying, "Oh yeah, today was the day you showed up at our house." Even so, it was Koyo's happiest memory.

What's more, Kazuki had heard a rumor that Koyo and his parents weren't even blood-related. They had only adopted him due to some unknown circumstances. Kazuki had never bothered to ask whether it was true or not. He didn't really see that it mattered much.

"I guess I was hoping for it. That we'd hear something on the other side of that white noise. Maybe I was just hoping it would be the beginning of something new."

"White noise..." Kazuki muttered, but his memories were foggy at best. "Hey, Koyo," he said instead. "What're you going to do next year?" He tried to anticipate the response.

"I'll leave this island."

"Really?"

"You, too, right?"

"Yeah."

"One more year," Koyo said. If he just endured one more year, he'd be free.

Kazuki thought about how, once he left the island, he would be certain to miss Koyo every now and then.

Kazuki and Koyo passed through the school entrance and opened up their respective lockers. There were five firmly sealed letter-like things inside Kazuki's.

"This doesn't look like postal mail," Koyo laughed. He had about ten letters in his box. "You, too, Kazuki?"

"Yep," he answered. But he knew what he had received and what Koyo had received were totally different things. Every single one of the envelopes Kazuki held in his hand was adorned with words like "CHALLENGE" or "TRIUMPH" scrawled in impassioned, messy handwriting. Koyo's, on the other hand, were sweetly decorated with hearts and such, with "To Kasugai-kun" written in soft lettering.

In general, Kazuki received what were known as letters of challenge.

Koyo received what were acknowledged worldwide as love letters.

"We both got more than usual," Koyo said

with an honest face. Kazuki shook his head in silence. It didn't seem like a fair comparison. The boys on this funless island were trying so hard to crush the boredom caused by all their pent up energy. Meanwhile, the island somehow seemed to nurture a sense of militarism.

"Somehow" meaning that, for some reason, there was a dojo on this island. It was a place which taught healthy young children how to fight safely using a style called *aikijujutsu*. They mainly taught things such as how to perform an ukemi roll, how to throw and be thrown without breaking bones, how to properly treat a sprain, how to expand the diaphragm if you were nailed in the solar plexus, and which vital locations on the body you should never attack. The owners of the dojo were a husband and wife. The husband was also a police officer, while the wife was a school physical education instructor.

Additionally, they had a daughter. She was in the same grade as Kazuki and quite attractive, making her fairly popular with the boys. But she had one common catch, which was that she wouldn't go out with anyone weaker than her. There was one person who had conquered this drawback completely without intending to.

It was Kazuki.

For some reason, she had taken it upon herself to help in instructing the boys' physical education class. Kazuki had accidentally used too much force in throwing her, thereby slamming her into the mat so hard that she almost blacked out. This was far from being a trigger for her falling for him. In fact, he seemed to remember her telling him something along the lines of "Someday, I'll kill you." But she never took her revenge on him, and they carried out their days peacefully. In place of that, however, he received a letter of challenge from a boy one day. With Kazuki having no idea what was going on, someone had laid out a mat in the gymnasium after school and challenged him, and Kazuki had won by a landslide. Kazuki later learned that this boy had had feelings for the daughter from the dojo, and that this was his desperate attempt to win her affection.

From this had spawned a great new pastime amongst a group of the boys. "Beat Kazuki, get a kiss," they would say. A truly wholesome activity.

Obviously, this didn't mean Kazuki would kiss the winner. They were referring to the daughter from the dojo. "Don't be stupid," she would say, rejecting the idea of being made a trophy, but the boys paid no mind. They came one after another to challenge Kazuki, and he defeated each and every one of them. Eventually, they forgot all about the dojo daughter, and beating Kazuki became their primary focus. Such is the way of young boys.

There was a silent agreement about the rules of these challenges. Challenges would be carried out on Saturdays after school, and no more than eight challenges could be held in a single day. Bets were limited to two thousand yen. The physical education committee representative would retrieve the key to the gymnasium from the teacher. The first challenger of the day would set out the mats. In general, challenges tended to occur at specific milestones, such as the beginning or end of the semester. In the time between, challengers were sure to be frequenting the dojo, honing their skills.

"Are you gonna go?" Koyo asked.

Kazuki casually stuffed the challenge letters in his bag. "If it's just five guys, it'll be over quick." If he tried to escape them, they would just chase him down anyway. Not the challengers, but the spectators. *I've got a whole month's allowance riding on you,* someone would say. *You're gonna send me to rags,* they'd whine. The thought of it was enough to convince Kazuki it was in his best interest to get it over with quickly.

"How about you, Koyo?"

"I'll read all these before the opening ceremony and decline them all within the day."

"All of them?"

"Well, you know how it is. Anyway, see ya," Koyo said, and went off up the stairs. He wanted to read over his letters on the school roof. He would commit the name and school year of each person to memory as he read their letters and come up with an appropriate, polite refusal for each one.

Why doesn't that guy just go out with one of them? Kazuki wondered as he headed to the gymnasium for the opening ceremony. He also wondered which was harder: denying the hearts of ten different girls simultaneously, or defeating challenger after challenger after school.

Surely, they were both hard. Just as the boys *needed* things like Ocean Baseball and challenges with Kazuki, the girls *needed* to make these confessions to Koyo. Romance was, after all, just another way to eliminate the boredom of this island.

Neither Koyo nor Kazuki could escape. That was what it all boiled down to. Maybe if Koyo just dated somebody, he'd stop being approached. But Maya had once spoken briefly regarding that.

"Kasugai-kun does like somebody," she had said. But for some reason, he couldn't confess his feelings. "Because that person might like someone else," she explained. It was all her intuition. But if Maya said it, it had to be true.

Kazuki knew it wasn't his place to talk. Why didn't he just lose a match? He should've just thrown a match right away. He should've been getting straight errors in Ocean Baseball, striking out, failing to steal bases. But surely these were things he couldn't allow. And it wasn't because it was disrespectful to his opponents. There was something inside him that simply wouldn't forgive the act of losing without exhibiting the best of one's ability. And that thing inside him was always there, telling him why he couldn't lose.

He headed towards the gym, observing the scene of students all over the place greeting each other. Nobody greeted him. "A little disappointed, but pretty relieved," he muttered, doing a direct impression of Maya. It pretty much described his current condition as the "secret weapon of the Western Slope," whose only greeting to the new semester was a bevy of challenge letters.

Those rows of windows casting light out onto the black ocean came to mind. That feeling of the freezing water from his dream. The feeling he had when he turned his back on that light. Why wasn't there a window where he belonged? Why did he have to leave the island in another year? Why did he have to lose?

He knew the answer to these questions. But it was only Maya to whom he was ever able to explain it.

One more year, he thought, like a prisoner counting down the days to freedom. He who had exerted so much effort to become a model prisoner was soon to be released. As though hoping nobody would try to talk to him, Kazuki entered the gymnasium and lay low in a corner.

Just then, a voice came from behind him. "Kazuki." For a moment, he couldn't turn around. "Long time no see, Kazuki." The voice called his name again. It almost seemed to be surrounding him. If Kazuki didn't turn around at this point, he would probably embarrass this person. But perhaps this person knew Kazuki would never do anything like that.

Kazuki turned around. "Soshi." The moment Soshi appeared before his eyes, his hands started to sweat. Soshi was surrounded by a large number of admirers. There were always lots of people, both male and female, dying to talk to him. This was due to his undiscriminating personality and the fact that he was the son of the mayor. This school was particularly modern, considering they were out in the middle of nowhere, and the nice facilities they had set up were largely thanks to the mayor.

"Good morning, Soshi," he finally responded. Kazuki thought to look him directly in the eyes, but he just couldn't maintain eye contact. He was completely distracted by Soshi's left eye. That scar that had robbed his eye of light, running from eyelid to cheek.

"Everyone, please excuse me," Soshi said gently, but with a tone that no one would dare object to. His fan club left him alone with Kazuki.

"Tell me more about Tokyo next time, Minashiro-kun!" a girl called back to him with blatant obsequiousness. Kazuki recalled that Soshi had gone off to Tokyo for spring break, which must've been why Kazuki had felt so at ease.

Soshi gave his crowd of groupies a gentle wave and smile and then walked over to Kazuki without ever looking back. "Haven't seen you in two weeks. Doesn't seem like you've gone through any drastic life changes, though."

"Yep." Kazuki tried to scoot back, but his feet were glued in place, so he just nodded.

"Did you check out the class rosters?" Soshi stuck his thumb in the direction of one of the corners of the room. On the wall was a list of all the classes and the names of the students in each one, but none of this was of interest to Kazuki. It was such a small student body anyway. His grade only had two classes. And, for the past few years, there was only one thing that ever concerned him: whether or not the boy before him right now would be in his class.

"We're in the same class, Kazuki. Let's have a good year," Soshi said with a smile. Kazuki felt that smile gripping his very heart.

"Wha—"

"What's wrong? Is that a bad thing?"

"Oh, no it's not, just—"

"Heh, I'm only kidding, idiot," Soshi grinned. Just like Koyo, there was something calming about his smile. But, unlike Koyo, there was something decidedly forceful about this calming effect. It was as though he was forcing Kazuki to calm down, to serve some specific objective.

"The same class..." Kazuki repeated with an upward glance at Soshi. For the last several years, he and Soshi had never been in the same class, even in elementary school. There were only two classes. A fifty percent chance of being put together. But for years they had remained separate, until Kazuki thought it must have been Soshi's will. If Soshi said he didn't want to be with Kazuki, he wouldn't be with Kazuki. That was the power of the position Soshi was in, just like his father. This was what Kazuki had come to believe.

However...

"We haven't been placed together in ages, huh?" Soshi said, sounding absolutely ecstatic.

"Yeah..." Kazuki wanted to ask him what he was getting at, but the words wouldn't come out. His throat had grown dry and raspy. He wondered if he was being punished for something. For thinking he just had one year to go. He felt like Soshi was telling him he could never escape.

"By the way, Kazuki, are you free tonight?"

For a split second, Kazuki didn't understand the question. "Free?"

"Can we hang out after a school for a bit? There's something I want to show you," Soshi said, sounding perfectly natural. And, in reality, there was no reason for him to sound unnatural. It was a fairly well known and accepted fact that Kazuki and Soshi had been friends since childhood.

This was because of their fathers' connection. Apparently, they had once been in the same line of work. Kazuki's father had parted with it after the death of his mother, but correspondence still occasionally came from Soshi's father, and every once in a while Kazuki's father would go to visit and not come home until late at night.

Why would his romanticist artist of a father be called over to the mayor's house? In time, Kazuki deduced through his father's conversations over the phone that the mayor probably trusted him and came to him for advice. Kazuki was dumbfounded. He couldn't help but wonder if this had something to do with how his father was able to make a decent living selling those weird ceramic dishes.

The sons of these two fathers who trusted each other so dearly naturally grew to be friends. For as long as they could remember, Kazuki and Soshi had often shared each other's company as their fathers got together and immersed themselves in conversation. Yes, there was certainly nothing awkward between them.

Except for the fact that this was the first time Soshi had spoken to him like this in a good five years.

"You want to show me something?"

"There's something I only want you to see. You've got to keep it a secret from everyone else," Soshi said, lowering his voice.

What the hell was this about? Kazuki could

feel the chaos bubbling. Why was Soshi treating him so special all of a sudden? And why at a place like this, just before the opening ceremony with everyone in the whole school present? He wished Maya had been there. He couldn't tell what Soshi was thinking. Were his intentions good or evil, or did he not have any? Even that was a complete mystery.

"I, uh...Well, I've got some stuff going on today, and..." The words just popped out of his mouth. He knew he was just running away like a coward. Soshi looked a bit surprised, as if the response had thrown him into confusion.

"Oh. Another challenge, or something?"

Now how did he know about that? Kazuki wanted to ask him, but Soshi cut him off with a snicker.

"Speaking of which, did I remember to place a bet?"

Suddenly Kazuki felt as though he'd been deeply betrayed. "Place a...How long have you..."

"I dunno. Since sometime last year, I guess."

It must have been around the time Kazuki had beaten the dojo girl. At this point, he became aware that he felt hurt. But why? Suddenly, he didn't seem to know anything about Soshi *or* himself. Talking to Soshi like this, he felt something he hadn't felt in years. But *what* exactly?

"If it's okay with you, I'll just go ahead and ask the challenger to change the day."

"Huh?"

"I mean, it wouldn't be right to just have you forfeit the match, right? Or if you *really* want to take on all these challengers today, we could always do this another time. What do you say?"

"I...I'll go if that's what you want. Just forget about my plans." The words naturally spilled out.

"Really? Okay, I'll go ahead and tell everyone," Soshi smiled. It was a smile that plainly declared, "Me and some of the other guys have been off somewhere getting our kicks at your expense." At last, Kazuki realized that this is what hurt him. At the same time, he vaguely understood what this was a sensation that he was feeling for the first time in years.

Soshi faced Kazuki with a smile and a gaze that hadn't changed in five years. The memory of a time when Kazuki had thought of him as a close friend came rushing back. His heart pounded like there was an alarm going off in his chest. It felt as though his most precious thing, a thing that once damaged would never stand on its own again, had suddenly become plain to see and fallen into another person's hands.

"What do you want to show me?"

Soshi stared at him in silence with one right eye and one scarred left eye. "Wait and see," he grinned. Just then, the school bell rang and teachers began calling for the students to line up. "Well, see you after school, Kazuki."

"Soshi."

"Yeah?"

"Who'd you bet on?"

"Who...?" Soshi mumbled, then grinned with a hint of embarrassment once he had grasped the meaning of the question. Who had he bet would win the match,

Kazuki or one of his challengers? Kazuki stared straight at him without breaking eye contact.

Soshi spoke. "After school, I'll tell you that, too."

And with that, he turned away. A moment later, the frantic sound of footsteps clamored into the room. "Ah, I made it!" Maya burst into the gymnasium. Shoulders heaving, she took note of Kazuki's' presence. "Hey, Kazuki-kun...and Minashiro-kun," she said as her eyes widened in shock.

Soshi glanced over at her and left to join the filing students without a word. In his place, Maya came and stood beside Kazuki. Her eyes stayed on Soshi.

"So you were talking to Minashiro-kun."

"Yeah."

"You'd better stop," she snapped.

"Huh?"

She turned to him. She looked as though she might cry any second. Kazuki was in the dark.

"Seriously, stop. I don't know what he told you, but don't ever listen to him," she pleaded.

Maya was in the other class. This, too, was something that hadn't happened in years. Unlike with Soshi, it was normal to Kazuki for them to be placed together.

At the end of the last class that day, Koyo, who had bee placed in Kazuki's class, came over to his desk. "Why the long face? Don't you have a big match after this?"

"Nah. Something else came up."

"Something else?"

"Yeah. How about you?"

"Three girls left," he said with a shrug. Between the opening ceremony and now, he had spent all of his time between each class dutifully visiting each girl and kindly rejecting them.

"It's a hard life, huh?" Kazuki truly felt sorry for him.

"So, how about you?" Koyo started to say, only to be interrupted by another voice.

"Kazuki. You ready?" Soshi hurried over to him as if trying to pass by before being swarmed by his fans. As if unable to defy him, Kazuki gave a silent nod.

Koyo was flabbergasted. "You mean you're doing something with Soshi?"

"Yeah." He recalled Maya's expression from before the opening ceremony. To be sure, part of him was saying that it wasn't too late. He could still duck out. But he stood up, mentally apologizing to Maya and that part of himself.

"Wow, this must be the first time in four years, seven months, and eleven days," Koyo said as he looked back and forth between the two.

"Since what?" Soshi asked.

"Since I've seen you two go home together," he answered with a gentle smile. Surely it was a genuine one. Seeing a pair who had once drifted apart for whatever reason now side-by-side going home together was certainly the kind of thing that would delight him. "I guess you always were buds, huh? Since you were little.

No wonder," he said with a look of satisfaction. Kazuki was amazed at the happiness it brought Koyo just to see people getting along.

"We've just got something to do," Soshi said dryly. "Let's go," he urged, and turned away from Koyo.

"You never know what opportunity will bring, buddy," Koyo said, giving Kazuki a pat on the back.

Kazuki and Soshi left the classroom. They remained in silence until retrieving their shoes from the shoe cupboard in the school entrance.

"Huh. So that's all?" Soshi mumbled.

"That's...all?"

Soshi just shrugged his shoulders without an explanation. He put on his shoes and headed for the gate. Kazuki followed behind obediently. Somehow he got the feeling that it would be better to just let Soshi do the talking. Otherwise he wouldn't be prepared to absorb whatever Soshi had to say.

"Kazuki-kun!" came a voice from behind them that resembled a scream. It was enough to make everyone in the vicinity turn to look.

"Tomi..." Kazuki uttered her name, though he didn't know what was happening. Maya stared back at him, a combination of terror mixed with pity written on her face. It was as though she thought he was about to die.

"Kazuki-kun, why?"

Even though she had warned him, her usually

sweet voice was suddenly filled with bitterness.

"Tomi, there's—"

There's nothing to worry about, he wanted to say, even though he had no basis for believing so. But, then again, she didn't have any basis either, he thought. But before he could speak, Maya ran up to him and shot a glare at Soshi. Her eyes had begun to tear up.

"Minashiro-kun! Where are you taking him?!" she screamed accusingly, without a hint of reserve or even an introduction. She was probably the only person in history to ever speak this way to Soshi, son of the mayor and head of the school. Trying to avoid getting involved, the surrounding students quickly distanced themselves from the three and continued watching in a big circle. All, including Kazuki and Maya, eagerly anticipated Soshi's response.

What are you talking about?

Surely it would be something to that effect. Or so everybody thought. But the next words out of Soshi's mouth betrayed the expectations of all those present.

"Savant Syndrome?" It sounded like nonsense. "You were able to gather that with just this tiny bit of information?"

Soshi's words had Kazuki—and probably most everyone else present—dumbfounded. But there was some subtle nuance in what he said that seemed to be confirming Maya's accusations.

In other words, he was trying to take Kazuki a place that he shouldn't be taking him. And evidently it was a place that Maya had to desperately try and stop Kazuki from going.

"Either way, this has nothing to do with you, Tomi. Don't get involved," Soshi said like a defiant adult.

At this point, Kazuki saw two things he had never seen before in his whole life.

One was Soshi, speaking with such coldness that it seemed to deny the other person's existence.

The other was Maya, so filled with unspeakable rage that her face had gone blue.

"Minashiro-kun...Are you going to kill him?" Her voice was dry and cracked with anger. She spoke so low that the surrounding people couldn't hear, but Kazuki was taken aback.

"Kill me?"

"No," Soshi answered readily. "I'm just going to raise the level of his awareness restriction code. There is a chance his current personality may alter as a result, but we're certainly not going to erase it, much less throw him into real combat." He spit out the words in a fumbled stream.

Maya knit her eyebrows, uncertain of what he was talking about.

"You mean you've just been going off intuition this whole time?" Soshi said. "So you're at the lowest level of awareness after all."

"L-lowest level? What's that supposed to mean?"

"It's just an expression used to define an absolute value. It's not something bad."

"I don't know what you're talking about. Explain all this!"

Kazuki was at the height of confusion. Soshi's behavior and Maya's anger were equally incomprehensible to him. And yet he was their sole topic of discussion.

"Soshi, where are we going?" he said in a timid attempt to break into their back-and-forth. He suspected that if Soshi just gave an answer, it would calm Maya down.

Soshi's face grew extremely bitter. "I can't believe the trouble has already started at this phase. The adults are gonna give me another damn talking to, with or without a report."

At last, he seemed to be acting his age as he filled with anxiety. Just as this occurred to Kazuki, Soshi looked his way. His right eye as well as his left eye, robbed of light, were both home to such determination and willpower that it overwhelmed Kazuki.

"Alvis," Soshi said.

"What's—?" Kazuki stopped himself short before finishing his question. Something immediately popped into his head.

The Dock.

Just that word. It was a giant storage facility, more than four times as big as this schoolyard. That was Alvis.

Rather, that was one part of Alvis. But why had the Dock popped into his head right away? Because that was most likely where Soshi was trying to take him. That facility was the only part of Alvis that Kazuki had anything to do with.

What? What was he thinking?

He couldn't recall a clear image. Only vague information rapidly swelling within his brain. He couldn't make heads or tails of what the information meant, and a frighteningly disturbing sensation gripped him. He could feel the hair standing on the back of his neck. The very word *Alvis* felt like an ultimate trigger, threatening to shake his reality. His head began to swim as his vision went black.

"Stop it," he groaned, stumbling off balance.

"Kazuki-kun?" Maya immediately grabbed him by the arm. At the same time, the entire vicinity filled with an incredible noise.

It was a siren, Kazuki realized, and suddenly his vision came back. Maya, gripping his arm with concern, and Soshi, who was looking up to the sky with a grim expression, came into view.

"W-what's going on? That's the emergency alarm." Maya was now *clinging* to his arm as she frantically scanned their surroundings. The other students stood frozen like deer in headlights as well.

A low groaning sound almost like a voice came echoing down from overhead. It was somehow clear what it was. It was distinctly different from the sound of the emergency alarm. It was the high alert sound used to signal the need for fast action.

"Where's it coming from?!" Kazuki frantically looked around the area in confusion. He was looking for the source of the noise, but it seemed to be coming from all over. It might have been sounding off throughout the entire town, or even the entire island.

"A siren alert at a time like this. This puts another dent in the plans," Soshi muttered bitterly. He gave up on watching the sky and began yelling into the crowd. "Everyone, get to the back of the schoolhouse!" Of course, all this did was raise a variety of confused reactions from his fellow students as they stared back at him. "This is an emergency evacuation! Hurry! Do you want to die?!" he continued shouting with uncontestable authority, and suddenly everyone's faces turned pale.

"Huh? What? Is there a tsunami coming?"

"Is it a volcano eruption?"

"I don't feel an earthquake..."

The crowd buzzed with concern as they gathered around him.

"Behind the schoolhouse! Call everyone!" Soshi continued yelling, grabbed Kazuki's wrist and started tugging on it. "Come on!"

Because Maya was on his other arm, they were pulled together.

"Everyone, escape to the back of the school! Hurry!" After the initial tug, Soshi soon let go of Kazuki. He seemed to have assumed Kazuki would just follow behind him, and in fact that was the case. Maya also released his arm, as if afraid of becoming a burden, but followed swiftly behind. "This way! Everyone, come to the back of the school!" Soshi continued shouting constantly as they moved.

When they arrived behind the school, everyone was in a state of complete bewilderment. The only things there were the fence surrounding the school grounds, the trees lining it, a bicycle parking lot on the other side, and a cistern. And it was hardly a place the entire student body could hope to fit into.

"I'm going to open the block now. Get back," Soshi said, making his way to the electrical power board in the corner on the back wall of the school. He produced a wallet from his pocket, and in turn produced a black card from the wallet. He took the liberty of opening the power board on his own and began operating the buttons with a satisfying clicking sound. In no time, a portion of the inside panel opened even further, revealing something similar to a card-operated payphone.

He inserted his card into it. The payphone was buttonless and had an electronic panel unlike anything Kazuki had ever seen, and yet Soshi operated it with utmost confidence and no hesitation as he extracted the miniature microphone.

"This is an emergency request. Please release Block W-3 from CDC. I can't open it from this side with my current authorization. Repeat: please release Block W-3 from CDC," he said into the microphone.

"Block W-3...The school?" came an irritated reply from a seemingly already too busy man. The voice came through some part of the electrical power board and reached the ears of the crowd. Up until now they had simply been watching him in silence, but the students began to grow nervous and wonder if Soshi himself wasn't in fact the most dangerous thing there. What in the world was he talking about? Wouldn't he get into big trouble with the teachers for tampering with that thing?

"Yes, I'll raise the awareness restriction codes

of everyone here to Level Three," Soshi said into the phone.

"Wait. That's currently an invalid section. CDC's current priority is mobilization."

"Then please request that invalid sections be immediately brought up to Type Two security alert! If we suffer casualties here, who's going to take the blame?!" Soshi punched the lid of the electrical power board as he shouted into the phone. It created an incredible noise. Soshi's sudden outburst of anger was so frightening that it made the crowd collectively jump.

Kazuki watched on in amazement. He had never seen Soshi acting so frantic before.

"Uh, understood. Wait five seconds." The person on the other end, most likely an adult male, seemed to have gotten flustered by Soshi's impassioned display of determination. By this point the number of students had more than doubled, and the crowd had sunk even deeper into confusion, uttering things like "I don't know what's what!" and "Isn't that the emergency alarm? What are we doing back here?"

Within that chaos, Soshi clearly stood out to Kazuki. There was no one there to help him. He had to single-handedly shoulder all of the responsibility. And no one here understood the struggle he was going through for them.

At last, a response came through the speaker. "Permission received from CDC. Block security alert raised to Type Two at current time."

"Thank you very much," Soshi said, his voice overflowing with honest gratitude.

"Confirming evacuation supervisor code number and block operation. It will open within seventeen seconds." With that, the voice cut out.

Soshi quickly returned the microphone to its original position, pulled out his card, and shut both lids to the power board. Then he turned to face everyone and spoke once again. "It's going to open."

At the same time, they could hear the sound of water and rumbling earth. Water flooded out of the cistern, the concrete began to crack, and the ground around the cistern began to noisily rend apart as something enormous emerged from within.

Kazuki and Maya stood stunned and said nothing. This all-too-sudden chain of events spurred a great outcry from the crowd. Some even tried to scramble away.

"This is the quickest route to the shelter! Everyone, get in!" Soshi's rousing cries brought everyone back together. Kazuki held his breath. Maya and everyone else did the same.

A piece of the front of the giant object moved downward, suddenly opening its mouth—its door. After a substantial moment of blankness, Kazuki at last realized this was an entrance. He seemed to suddenly recall something called a "pit dwelling" that he had once learned about in one of his classes. This was very much the same type of thing, only with a round entrance made of blackish metal.

"We're supposed to go in here?" Maya whimpered. Her uneasiness made its way to Kazuki and infected him as well. With the high alert signal blaring, this weird structure appearing behind the school, and Soshi sputtering things that didn't make any sense, everyone was on the brink of panic. They were gripped by a deep terror. It was a situation no one had ever experienced before, and they had no idea how to react. But within all this Soshi stood alone, shouting things no one understood.

"Without panicking, organize yourselves into three-person lines and enter through here! There's plenty of time for all of us to escape!"

But no one attempted to move. Their eyes stayed trained on him as if to say, "*You* go in first." Soshi began to look frustrated. Just looking at him was enough to make you feel pity.

We have to go—Kazuki was suddenly gripped by a strong sense of obligation. If he just started moving, everyone else would follow. But if someone didn't have faith in Soshi, they'd all just stay frozen like this. He ground his back teeth and walked up to Soshi.

"Kazuki-kun..." Maya said when she saw him. In a panic she clutched onto his arm. Soshi began yelling even more, when suddenly...

"We'll be safe if we go in here, Soshi?" Koyo emerged to the head of the crowd, speaking in a voice so cheerful it almost seemed like he had shown up at the wrong place. Next to him was a girl who looked to be his junior and who was crying for some reason.

"That's right. This is the only safe place," Soshi confirmed.

Koyo turned to the girl beside him. "Let's go in," he said comfortingly. "Watch your step."

"Kasugai-senpai, I...I like..."

"Let's discuss that later on, okay? Right now let's worry about your safety. 'K?'" Evidently he had been in the middle of turning the girl down when all of this began. The girl nodded with tears in her eyes. She and Koyo stepped through the entrance with no further hesitation. Soshi, Kazuki, Maya, and everyone else were dumbfounded, but soon people began moving.

"I...I'm going too."

"If Koyo's going, I'm going."

Kazuki and Maya were eventually swallowed up by the crowd and approached the entrance.

"Soshi, what about you?"

"You go first, Kazuki. The enclosure should form a path to the shelter," Soshi said, and proceeded to run to the back of the mob.

Kazuki was immediately struck by a sense of uneasiness. The one person they could rely on, probably the only person who could explain all this, was gone.

"What's the 'shelter'?" Maya mumbled. Kazuki wanted to ask Soshi the same question, and that probably went for everyone else present. Kazuki let himself be pushed forward by the moving mob and began to descend the staircase without taking time to wonder what this uneasy feeling was.

The staircase led to a path lit by blue-white light. Floor, walls, and ceiling alike were constructed of sleek metal. Once moving, it was hard to stop a mob this size, so Koyo and his junior led them onward through the arcing corridor.

Eventually they came to a wall with a large entrance in it.

"Is this...?"

Koyo took point and passed through the entrance. It led to a wide open, illuminated room several times the size of the school gymnasium. The wall was entirely curved, forming a dome-like shape, and lined with doors and unfamiliar panels. There was also something that appeared to be an air purifier and an air conditioner with its vents open.

"Is this...the shelter?" Maya whispered as she edged into the room.

"Looks like it."

Kazuki entered as well, and suddenly felt relieved. The realization that this was a safe place had finally dawned on him. He wasn't sure why he thought so, but for the time being he let out a sigh of relief.

It suddenly occurred to him that there was a digital screen embedded in one of the walls of the entrance, frantically displaying something.

"It's our names, Tomi..."

Indeed, Kazuki and Tomi's names were displayed on the upper part of the screen, followed by a string of meaningless letters and numbers. The names popped in one after another and then scrolled down the screen. At the same time, a number in the upper right corner got larger and larger.

"Is this showing who has come into the room?" Maya whispered with great uneasiness as she looked at the screen. This uneasiness once again made its way to

Kazuki, spoiling his newfound sense of relief.

"Looks like it."

"Who's doing this?"

"What do you mean 'who'?"

The droves of people entering the dome structure clung together in groups and chattered about or else knocked on the walls. "This door's gotta be the toilet, and this one looks like a kitchen," they'd holler. "Here's the bath." Nobody had called roll or anything, so there was no way somebody could've entered all these names into a computer.

"It's got to be automatic," Kazuki said in an attempt to suppress his anxiety.

Maya shook her head. "That's...It's not like it's just the number of people. It's got our names too. How does it know? It's creepy."

"Creepy?"

"Is it our clothes? Our bags? But some people aren't carrying one. Shoes? No...Could it be our bodies? Eww..." Maya looked like she was about to cry. Kazuki screwed up his courage so he wouldn't be pulled in by her anxiety.

"What's so creepy about it?"

"It's like those thingies."

"Thingies?"

"At the supermarket register."

"Wha?"

"You know, where they beep the product and it shows you the price..."

"The barcode?"

"Yeah, that." Maya gave a nod. It suddenly

dawned on Kazuki why she thought this was so strange. In order for a machine to automatically determine who had entered the room, it would've needed some type of indicator or mark telling it who was who. If it was something on their clothes or personal belongings, it was no big deal. But if it wasn't...

"There must be something attached to our bodies. Where? This is creepy..." The sight of Maya restlessly rubbing her shoulders and arms brought forth the anxiety Kazuki had already once suppressed. At the same time, he felt words traveling through his mind as if to combat said anxiety.

"In the back of your shoulders. Right side for boys, left side for girls."

In fact, these words brought great peace to Kazuki. He wanted to share this peace with Maya. "In your left shoulder. Here." He poked her in the shoulder with his finger.

Maya flinched. "K...Kazuki-kun?"

"It doesn't do any harm."

"A panopticon for keeping track of the locations of individuals during an emergency—"

"It only works inside facilities like this within Alvis. It's not like it knows where you are all the time. I think we can just relax, Tomi."

"Wh...What are you saying?"

"Huh?"

"A...Alvis? What is that?" Maya said. Kazuki realized he didn't know how he knew any of this. To be sure, it was very strange. Why was he so relaxed now?

Suddenly an eardrum-shattering shriek rose up

from the crowd. "What are you talking about?! Quit saying all this creepy stuff!"

Another person raised their voice in protest. "I'm telling you, it's been bumped up to a Type Two Security Alert. That siren was to signal an assault from—"

"Get away from me! You freak!"

Kazuki and Maya watched in amazement. Similar things were beginning to happen all throughout the dome.

"We're in Alvis' W-3 shelter now, and—"

"They're coming from out of the sky."

"It's okay, we're underground now so they won't be able to read our thoughts. Don't worry."

Some people uttered incomprehensible things, others lashed out at them in response.

"What the hell are you talking about?! You're being freaky! You're all nuts!"

"I don't want to hear this crap, so shut up, will you?!"

"You guys have all cracked!"

Gradually, the crowd separated itself into two big groups: those who understood and those who were completely confused. But, eventually, the side that understood began to increase more rapidly.

"I...see. So this is the lowest echelon of Alvis." It was as if some invisible force was quickly engulfing the entire room. Kazuki stood in astonishment while Maya gaped at the crowd beside him.

"Everyone's changing into different people." She wondered if she, too, would start to change, and slowly began edging away.

Just then, a stern voice emerged from the entrance. "What were you thinking, bringing everyone here before their awareness restriction codes had averaged out? You could've caused a panic."

"If we had waited for them to average out, we wouldn't have been able to respond to the threat. It was a bit rash, but it was the appropriate course of action."

"A bit?" The person bumped into Maya from behind. "Oh, sorry," she said. Beside her was Soshi, evidently done bringing people in.

"K...Karin-chan?" Maya uttered the girl's name and edged away from her slightly.

"Maya-chan, it's okay. You know, your face is totally pale."

Unable to tell the girl it was her fault, Maya instead just shook her head in silence.

Kuramae was this girl's name as Kazuki knew it. They'd been placed in the same class a few times, and she was usually made the class representative due to her stable character. Kazuki seemed to recall that she used to go by the nickname of "Mom." Come to think of it, he could remember having seen her talking to Soshi a number of times at school. He had always assumed they were going to each other for advice as fellow class representatives or something.

"Maya-chan's code isn't following suit. You know that girls are more likely to undergo mental trauma when you change the codes. Can you fix her, Minashiro-kun?"

Always ready to dish out a scolding. How very "Mom"-like, Kazuki thought, perhaps inappropriately.

"Don't worry, Maya-chan. Don't bother going out of your way to accept this. It's okay to believe strange things are strange," Kuramae said as she rubbed Maya's back. Soshi appeared to be suppressing his own emotions as he watched them.

Kazuki, meanwhile, wondered if Kuramae wasn't a bit wrong. To be fair, Soshi had talked down to an adult and gotten the entrance open for the sake of everyone's safety. Wasn't it a bit cruel to demand any more of him? The way Kuramae spoke to him seemed to reek of an "all or nothing" sort of attitude.

Not fully clear how much of this was his own personal judgment, Kazuki nevertheless decided to have a talk with Soshi. He wanted to ask what was going on. What was happening to all of them? How could he get rid of this feeling of anxiety? But before he could speak, someone else interrupted.

"So we're at ninety percent," Koyo said as he approached the electronic display by the entrance. The girl who had been crying was now sitting off in a corner somewhere with some classmates. "Soshi, what about the people who went home?" Kazuki saw Soshi shrug a bit. It wasn't like he could've followed them all. People sure expected a lot of him.

"The security alert level has been increased for the entire region. The adults in the area will guide everyone. The same goes for the elementary school. Alvis has the whole island at a Type Two Security Alert. "

Koyo looked at Soshi with a perplexed expression. "Sorry...I only understood about half of what you just said."

"Ahh..."

"It feels like a voice has been going through my head teaching me all these different things. Are you doing that, Soshi?"

"No, not me. Knowledge restrictions have been released according to each individual person's differences."

"Knowledge? When did we learn all this?"

"Fundamental hypnotic learning begins at around age six, but the greater part of it is from age thirteen onward."

"Hypnotic...? Huh?"

"Don't worry about it. You'll understand soon enough." Kazuki sensed something sinking in Soshi's voice. As if he wanted everyone else to learn the truth that only he knew, but at the same time knew this was something he shouldn't hope for.

"Ah!" Suddenly Maya shouted out. She dashed over to the electronic screen.

"Hey, Minashiro-kun. Does this thing know about other places too?"

"Other places?"

"Like where other people are."

"Other people? Are you looking for someone?"

Maya gave a big nod. When she had remembered this person, Maya had become completely able to accept her current situation. Somehow, Kazuki could tell. These unbelievable circumstances were difficult to accept on one's own. But once you had someone else with you, it was possible. Just as Soshi, Maya, and Koyo were there for Kazuki.

"Shoko. Shoko Hazama," Maya said. "I think she's at home, because her mom's still at work." Come to think of it, Kazuki remembered Maya once telling him that Shoko didn't have a father. She was alone.

"Please move aside." Soshi came up to the screen. He inserted the same black card from before into a slot below. The surrounding wall opened up and an operating screen appeared. He quickly typed in the name "Shoko Hazama."

"Wait, you're going to search the whole island for her?" Kuramae interrupted. Soshi nodded silently without looking away from the screen. "Hey, you don't have the authority to make such a breach of privacy like that with the management system."

"This is an emergency situation," Soshi said, writing her off. At the same time, a numerical value most likely indicative of Shoko Hazama's location appeared on the screen.

"Where is this? Shoko's house?"

"Probably. I've never been to the Hazama residence, but..."

"There's no doubt," Koyo said. Everybody looked to him. "It's actually easier for me to tell when you express it in numbers like that," he laughed. Kazuki was truly amazed by his ability to have a sense of humor in a situation like this.

Maya nodded once. "I'm going to Shoko's place."

"Maya-chan, no!" Kuramae scrambled to stop her.

"Why? We all came here because it's dangerous

outside, right? We have to escape, right? I can't just leave Shoko."

"A Type Two Security Alert essentially means 'stand by for an assault,'" Kuramae explained in frustration. It was obvious that Maya didn't understand.

"I just have to bring her here, right?"

"I said no! You'll be disobeying an order!"

"Why?! That's crazy!" Maya screamed. Kuramae began to get flustered.

"I'll go, too. We can't just let a girl go on her own," Koyo said, dutifully raising his hand.

"Wouldn't it be better if Koyo and I went and brought Shoko back?" Kazuki interrupted. Somehow, he felt it was the right thing to do. He was against the idea of Maya going outside. If there was anyone he wanted to be in a safe place, it was her. He wondered if this whole incomprehensible fiasco wasn't due to his going off with Soshi instead of listening to her in the first place.

"No means no. That goes for all of you," Kuramae said, trying to convince them.

Soshi stepped to the front. "It's fine. Let's go rescue Hazama." Maya's face immediately brightened.

"Minashiro-kun!! Exactly how far do you intend to overstep your bounds?!"

"It's evacuation combined with reconnaissance. We have to observe the tactical situation in order to request engagement of Waffeladen. It'll end up being a post-report, but it's not an infringement." To Kazuki, Maya, and Koyo, this was a barrage of nonsensical phrases. But Kuramae was immediately startled and took a step back. Her face wore a vivid expression of terror.

"Do you realize what you're saying?"

"Eventually it'll come to that. Based on what I saw outside this island, it's a sure thing. Time to take the initiative."

"That's...Do you plan on launching the system?! A pilot hasn't been selected yet!"

"It's exactly that kind of hesitation that the enemy has exploited every time to annihilate our forces!"

"Even if we don't fight, the Welle Shield will protect us!"

"The reactor won't be running at full capacity for another twelve days. It can't form a substantial barrier at this point. What do you think it meant when the siren went off today?!"

"The enemy...they're reading our thoughts...?"

"Either that, or they've predicted our actions through advanced mathematics. Either way, it's only a matter of time before we raise it up to Waffeladen."

It was all Maya and Koyo could do to try and follow along with Soshi and Kuramae's back-and-forth. But the mention of the word "enemy" sent a distinct chill up Kazuki's spine. It felt like something was suddenly trying to reveal itself inside him. He tried to consider what they had run to this shelter to get away from in the first place, and it filled him with terror. But it was this terror that drove him.

Kuramae cast a glance at him. "What about a pilot then? Don't tell me you're going to use Makabe-kun."

Chill. Kazuki was covered in goosebumps. Pilot?

What was she talking about? Though he didn't understand it, the fear nevertheless swelled inside him. Soshi, perhaps aware of Kazuki's feelings, nodded straight at him.

"Depending on our orders. I was planning on showing Kazuki that very thing today."

"But—" Kuramae grew speechless. Kazuki felt a very strong impact, the kind that threatened to make his vision go black. Why he was feeling this he didn't know. But he was suddenly starting to understand where Soshi had been planning to take him and why Maya was trying so hard to stop him.

She stood next to Kazuki, smoldering with concern for Shoko. Koyo knit his brow, trying to somehow comprehend this conversation. Kazuki, meanwhile, wanted to say something to Soshi but couldn't figure out what.

"Of course, if the orders call for it, we'll use you, Kuramae."

"M-me?"

"It's just that Kazuki has the higher code constitution. It'll probably be Kazuki."

There was an incredible crunching noise. It was Kuramae grinding her teeth. It was the first time Kazuki had ever seen a girl display her aggression or warlike spirit or what-have-you in plain sight like that.

"Minashiro-kun, I'm at the same awareness level as you, and we've gone through the launch test over and over together. I've even undergone true combat training. Are you just—"

"I know. But orders will probably go for Kazuki."

"So, what, you're just going to do it that way

before you even *receive* the orders?"

"I'm responding to a situation."

"You're just scared, Minashiro-kun. That's why you want Kazuki by your side."

Soshi didn't answer. Kazuki once again felt like things were being taken too lightly. Their most vital things were also the most vulnerable, and they were all in each other's hands.

Surely, Soshi had said the most hurtful thing possible to Kuramae, and she had said the most infuriating thing back, and something equally compelling was now approaching Kazuki himself. He tried to brace himself for the coming sensation.

"Fine then, I'll go. To Shoko-chan's place," Kuramae said, her glance cast downward. "I'll go see if there's anything requiring a response."

Soshi gave a silent nod.

At the same time, Kazuki was struck by the sensation that he was being forced to a point of no return. Something fearsome, the source of all his anxiety, was swift approaching and asking no questions in the process. And the realization that there was nowhere to run engulfed him.

Can I accept this? he thought as he stared at Soshi's face. If he couldn't accept it, it would spell his immediate collapse. He would be greeting the end without ever even knowing why. Without ever understanding how things had ended up this way. It would just end.

Such an incredible feeling gripped him.

Chapter Two
Destination Through The Dark

Chapter Two
Destination Through The Dark

"Everyone please stay here. The adults will be here soon," Soshi said and exited the shelter. Kazuki, Maya, Koyo, and Kuramae followed after him. Soshi worked the panel by the entrance one more time and it closed, completely cutting off the voices of the students inside as they pleaded, "When do we get to go home?" and "I want to call my house."

"Let's go," Soshi said. Doing as they were told, the four hastily followed behind. Kazuki wondered if they were going back to the school the way they came, but they were not.

"The school's already deserted, so that way in has been sealed off. Besides, it's quicker to travel directly through Alvis than to take the town streets." Indeed, it did seem like it would be faster to travel on a straight path underground than to deal with the town's winding, elaborate streets, hills, and stone staircases.

"Earlier, before we entered the shelter, this place was shut off, wasn't it?" Koyo asked. Apparently, the walls could open and close, changing the underground path. "Is it possible to get locked in?" he asked.

"Don't worry. I just closed one of the barriers to lead everyone to the shelter earlier," Kuramae said.

"I've requested passage through the quickest route to the zone Hazama's house is in, so there's nothing to fear. In the unlikely event that we do somehow get trapped in, I can open it," Soshi said.

"Shoko..." Maya whispered to herself. Kazuki continued on beside her in silence.

Dock.

The word—the idea—grew bigger and bigger inside him, but no specific thoughts came to mind. Only random knowledge such as what direction it was in and what its purpose was.

Pilot.

The word that had come up in Kuramae and Soshi's conversation. Kazuki felt he probably should have asked about it, if only because they had mentioned him. But he couldn't even formulate a question. There was just something terribly ominous about the word. In reality, he didn't want anyone to ever bring it up again. He just prayed that he would have the right to choose— the right to run away—even if his prayers were in vain.

"We're going to exit to the outside here," Soshi broke away from the path, proceeding up a staircase—a metal staircase, like you might see on the inside of a submarine, or something. Near the exit, he once again used the black card to operate a control panel. An instant later, the area was flooded with light. The door opened with a thunderous noise, and Soshi led the way out.

Outside, green light burst into their eyes. It was a hill. Part of the slope was hollowed out, with a gaping wide mouth. Because the entrance had opened, chunks of the earth around it had cracked.

"It's Shoko's house," Maya said. They could see a Western-style house down below between the trees. It became apparent that they had traveled in such a straight line that it would've simply been foolish to travel the usual route from school.

"Shoko." Maya began to descend the hill's stone staircase.

Just then, something pitch black traveling along the shoreline came into view with a piercing noise. Maya stopped in her tracks. Kazuki and Koyo gasped in surprise. A countless number of gigantic chunks of pitch black steel appeared, making a sound like a gigantic caterpillar. They lined themselves up on the road and aimed their gun barrels out to sea with a great howl.

"T-tanks," Koyo said, hesitating over whether that was, in fact, the right name for them.

Soshi immediately bent himself forward between two trees to get a view of the area. "They've deployed a land unit here to form a pincer attack formation with the Intercept System on the adjacent island."

Kuramae, standing diagonally behind him, turned pale and shook her head. "But that...The town will...Is the enemy really going to come so close?"

"Enemy?" Kazuki said, almost unconsciously. He felt like if he didn't say something—*anything*—the incredible anxiety would have him screaming. The Kazuki who had lived out his days in sublime serenity was long gone. But evidently, he had spoken up at the exact moment when everyone had grown silent. They all turned to look at him, making it awkward.

"What...what do you mean?" he continued

timidly, as if to downplay the question. But the question didn't merit downplaying. Indeed, you could say he had hit the key issue.

"Yeah, what do you mean 'enemy'? Is some country attacking us?" Koyo asked, looking back and forth between Soshi and Kuramae.

"Is it a war?" Maya asked, expressing her own concerns. She wanted to hurry down the steps, but, at the same time, the bizarre sight of a nearby road completely lined with tanks was far too overwhelming.

"Yes, it is," Soshi said.

Kazuki, Maya, and Koyo all simultaneously felt like something cold had run them through the chest. Mortified by Soshi's words, they shared an indignant look at him but said nothing.

"But...it's not a country," he added and quickly proceeded past Maya and began to descend the stairs. He moved swiftly, as if the tanks might start shooting in their direction at any moment. The rest of the group scrambled after him.

"Not a country? What does that mean?" Koyo said after finally recovering from the shock as he tried to catch up with Soshi.

A tremendous roar rumbled above them. They all looked toward the sky to see a fleet of planes like missiles with wings attached flying toward the northern end of the island.

"They've deployed the defensive air force. Let's go." Soshi got to the bottom of the steps and broke into a sprint. No one else spoke. Two streets ahead there was a convoy of tanks, battle planes were soaring through the sky, and every house seemed empty. Looking around, they realized that shelter entrances similar to the one at school had popped up all over the sides of streets and in empty areas.

Kazuki felt his heart cry out. Excitement was about to engulf him. Realizing this would likely lead to panic, he desperately tried to contain himself as he ran onward.

Maya made her way to the exquisite Western-style porch of the Hazamas' home without any hesitation. "Shoko! Are you here?!" She banged on the door without bothering to try the bell. Then, frantically, she went for the knob. In that exact instant, the door opened inward from the other side.

"Maya." A slender girl appeared and Maya embraced her with tears in her eyes. She squeezed her so hard it almost looked like the girl would break.

"Shoko, you must've been scared being all alone. I'm sorry I took so long," Maya said, holding her by the shoulders.

Shoko shook her head and spoke in an ephemeral voice like a musical instrument crafted out of glass. "I knew I had to go because the entrance to Alvis opened, but I was scared, and..." she said. Kazuki heard it too, clear as day.

"Al...vis?"

"Yeah. Hm?" Shoko noticed the strange look of betrayal on Maya's face. "Maya? What's wrong? Did I say something weird?"

"Uh, no. Let's go. Put on your shoes, okay? Can you walk?"

Shoko gave a relatively energetic nod, considering her condition, and put on her shoes with audible effort. It seemed that the very act of going outside required her to exert herself quite a bit.

"Well, let's get going. Everyone's here with us."

"Everyone?"

They took one step from the porch toward the gate, and this time Shoko was the one to stop in her tracks. Kazuki and the other three had been watching from outside the gate all this time.

"Ah..." Shoko uttered with a start and froze, like an ice doll that would shatter to bits if it moved even an inch. Her normally pale, almost blue face, had suddenly turned bright red. "Mayaaa," she whimpered, looking at Maya with eyes filled with tears entirely different from Maya's own tears moments before.

"Uh...yeah." Maya gave a troubled nod to indicate that she knew what Shoko was thinking.

"Why are they...But I'm dressed like this..." She pulled her jacket closed. It seemed she was only wearing pajamas underneath. She tried to slink backwards, but Maya frantically snatched hold of her.

"It's okay. You don't look weird. Anyway, let's hurry."

"But, I didn't think anybody would be here, so I didn't change, and—"

Her already weak voice was immediately blotted out by a distant sound similar to thunder.

"What was that?! Did one of the tanks fire?!" Koyo whipped his head around.

Soshi answered right away. "No, the defensive air force has begun to engage the enemy. We have to hurry, or this'll get bad."

"Shoko-chan, can you run?" Kuramae shouted. Shoko stammered and hesitated to answer, but it was obvious that there was no way she could.

Another clap of thunder rang out. Startled, Kazuki's eyes shot skyward.

"Kazuki-kun!" Maya shrieked. She was at the height of desperation. Kazuki's eyes shot back towards Maya.

"Me?"

"Carry!"

"Carry?"

"You're a guy, right?!"

"Sure I am, but carry what?"

"Here ya go," Maya said, and gave Shoko a light shove towards him. Shoko's eyes went wide like a cat after its tail is stomped on. Kazuki froze, and Koyo at last understood what was going on.

"Hey now..." Just as Kazuki tried to say something, an unbelievable thing happened right in their midst. As the thunderous claps continued to ring out, enormous walls shot up out of the roads here and there. The number of walls rapidly increased right before their eyes, until the whole town was virtually surrounded like a building.

"The mainland has switched to Waffeladen," Soshi muttered. There was something horribly foreboding about it as it fell upon the ears of all those present.

And that wasn't the only surprise.

The sudden appearance of the walls caused the surrounding area to grow darker, and the shadows began moving together. It looked like a gigantic sundial. The shadows stretched from right to left at an alarming speed. It was as if time had sped up and was about to take those present into a completely different future—a completely different world.

"The sun..." Maya looked up at the sky, dumbfounded. The sun was waning quickly. Even the clouds and the color of the sky seemed to have been completely wiped away somehow.

"The sky...it's changing." No sooner had Koyo spoke than the sun completely disappeared. But the light remained. A moment later, it had reappeared in the opposite side of the sky. Also there were the clouds and sky that had just disappeared.

"What is this?! What's happening?!" Kazuki let out a scream filled with confusion and dread, possibly the first time in his entire life.

"The sky has flipped," Koyo answered in disbelief.

"They've removed the mirrored camouflage to acquire energy for generating the Welle Shield," Soshi explained flatly. Naturally, it was beyond everyone's comprehension.

Only Kuramae kept her eyes on the sky as if she was expecting something. "As long as they generate the shield—"

"It will be breached," Soshi said, shattering her expectations. Just then, the sound of a fast-growing number of explosions thundered around them. One after another they came, so harsh that they seemed to rattle the very air.

"The enemy has made contact with the shield! Run if you don't want to die!" Soshi shouted between explosions. Somehow they managed to hear him. "Kazuki, if you're going to carry her, then do it!"

The urgency in his voice made Kazuki jump into action as if he had been lashed with a whip.

"Eh!" Shoko cried as he lifted up her delicate stem of a body. It was nothing compared to that fifteen-level stack of chairs he had to move during last New Year's big cleaning. He almost looked like a prince carrying his princess through a threshold, but in reality he was closer to a rescue medic on the frontlines.

"Hey, Kazuki—" Koyo started to say, but cut himself off when he noticed Shoko clutching Kazuki's neck in surprise. Meanwhile, Soshi was already waving for everyone to get moving as he charged onward. Kuramae, Koyo, Maya, and Kazuki with Shoko in tow ran after him. As they dashed through the maze that this forest of walls had created, the booming cacophony grew harsher and harsher. The target of their search—an entrance into Alvis—was nowhere to be found. It seemed they had all been sealed off already.

Soshi placed his hand against the walls here and there, muttering "No, this isn't it" several times. But before the others' anxiety could reach its peak, he finally found what he was looking for. He placed his hand on the thin side of one of the walls—which in itself was thick enough to be called another wall—and found a lid. He slid it down and smashed his hand against the button underneath. A piece of the wall opened up, revealing an entrance. Soshi gestured for them to go inside.

Just then, the noise stopped, leaving their thoroughly pummeled eardrums ringing.

Silence.

It was as though all sound had been sucked out of the world.

Suddenly, they could hear white noise. It could have been the broadcasting speakers laid throughout the city, or it could have been a television from a nearby home. It could have even been a radio cassette player or a set of Walkman headphones. But, soon enough, anything and everything capable of emitting sound was releasing the same ear-shattering white noise.

Everyone stood frozen, bathing in the flood of sound. Soshi stared up at the sky, his eyes full of determination. Kuramae pushed herself up against the wall, her face full of horror, and Koyo stood and listened to the noise with his eyes peeled. Maya just clutched the front of her blouse while Shoko clung to Kazuki with all her might and her eyes shut.

Kazuki was watching Soshi. That day, seven years ago—on March 31st, according to Koyo. He could remember that Soshi was one of those children circled around that silver radio.

An instant later, the noise ceased. Complete silence had fallen upon them once again. And then, it happened.

"Are you—"

The voice was painfully clear, as if it were stroking their very hearts.

"—Are you there?"

That was its question.

Terror raced through Kazuki's entire being. It felt like something had just gone inside him. It was like his mind had reflexively answered the question he had just been posed. And in so doing, it had been captured. That was how he felt.

"Run!" Soshi shouted at the top of his lungs and gestured towards the entrance. His eyes were practically burning a hole through the sky. They were trained on something far up in the distance, something that was descending toward them, radiating incredible brilliance.

Everyone gasped. It wasn't out of fear. They were simply bedazzled, to a point of trembling. For a moment, Kazuki wondered if God had just appeared. Such was the unspeakable beauty of this luminescence now flooding the earth.

The golden light shined so brilliantly that it seemed to paint the whole sky. In the very center of it was an object somehow evocative of a human being, like a pulsating jewel brought to life. Near the center of the object, it sparkled in a rainbow of hues. The more you gazed into its reflection, the more it would suck you in.

Everybody stared at it in awe. The more they bathed in the object's golden glow, the more tranquil they became, and soothing music so soft it was barely even there seemed to be flowing through the air.

It was the terrible sound of an endless bombardment that brought them back to their senses. Maybe the tanks along the coast had begun firing in unison. At the same time, the thunderous sound of explosions rang out from all over the island. There must have been firefights occurring all over the place. It seemed those tanks weren't the only ones going at it.

The shimmering golden presence was basked in smoky explosions without marring its own beauty with so much as a scratch. Meanwhile, something in its hands began to expand.

Kazuki could have sworn he saw something pitch black wriggling behind the golden presence. An instant later, there was such a thunderous clamor that overwhelmed even the gunfire of the tanks. It wasn't the sound of an explosion. It was the sound of something hard being smashed to bits by a great force.

"What's happening?!" Koyo shouted, as if only now able to muster a voice. There was a wall in the way, blocking their view of the coastline. Or so it seemed, when suddenly it happened.

At first sight, it appeared to be some kind of gigantic black sphere. It was spinning at an incredible speed, sucking in anything in its path and stripping the nearby trees of their leaves. It wasn't that someone had thrown this spherical object—it had just *appeared* there all of a sudden.

In a matter of seconds, the rotating blackness had swallowed everything within it and disappeared. Everything in the area was engulfed by the sphere.

It hadn't been destroyed—it had *disappeared.* Walls, houses, streets; they had all been erased in single instant, leaving nothing more than a sphere-shaped crater in their place.

Everyone but Soshi and Kuramae was so gripped with fear that all they could do was scream incoherently. This was totally different from a bomb explosion, and it spurred within them a fear of the unknown—of being *erased.*

"I've never seen the Wurm Sphere before," Kuramae said, her face written over with pure fear. "Even a Fafner would be doomed if it took one of those..."

"If it entered Assimilate Mode, it could defend itself against a distortive rotating body by sacrificing its outer shell," Soshi said, in an attempt to extinguish her fears. "Why don't you think about the units that don't even have an Assimilate Mode function? Why do you think we've gone through so many launch tests? To start doubting the abilities of the Fafners?"

It seemed his last remark had only served to turn Kuramae's fear into anger. "I don't need a backseat pilot like you to tell me that!!" Her voice was more cutting than a knife.

"Good, then. The enemy is still searching the area, so hurry up and get inside. We'll split into two groups," Soshi's manner of speaking remained aloof, but this time he guided the group into Alvis personally. The entrance shut behind them, cutting off the golden glow and the sounds of gunfire completely. The sense of relief was incredible.

Kazuki realized that he was desperate to get back to the shelter. At the same time, he was aware that part of him was afraid it was already too late to go back. But in his heart, he knew that there was no option but to press onward.

"Two groups?" Koyo asked after they descended the stairs and came to the main path.

"I'll take you guys as far as the CDC. It's the battle command post. Kuramae, go with Kazuki and head for the Dock."

A chill shot up Kazuki's back. The Dock—so someone had finally brought it up. There was no running from it now. He was going there.

"You really want me to take him there?" Kuramae replied with a certain sternness.

Soshi gave an indifferent nod. "You won't be the one getting inside it. He will."

"Don't be ridiculous! Do you want to kill him?!"

"Kuramae, you are a test pilot. Don't forget that. Now hurry, there's no time."

"H-how *dare* you—" Kuramae took a step towards him but was cut off by someone else.

It was Maya. She stepped in front of Soshi and stared him straight in the eye with her trademark "I think I get it" gaze. In reality it only lasted for a few seconds, but the silence that had suddenly fallen upon the Alvis path seemed to stretch out much longer.

"Rabbit," Maya said. It was one of her typically vague decipherings of a situation, but also a signal of her understanding.

"What—?" Soshi furrowed his brow at her, but she just took a step back and shook her head sadly.

"Nothing. Kazuki, thanks for what you did for Shoko."

Kazuki gave her a confused look before realizing that he had, indeed, been carrying her friend. "Can you walk?" he asked Shoko, still lying in his arms.

"Uh, I, um...Yes," she said, her bright red face hung in embarrassment. She nodded repeatedly as he let her down. Koyo simply gave a small shrug as Maya came to her side to accompany her.

"Soshi," Kazuki said. There was nothing deep on his mind. Only one simple question. "Me?" he whispered.

Soshi began to speak but cut himself off. Kazuki imagined he was going to say that he never thought it would come to this or apologize for not having an explanation. But holding back all such responses, Soshi only nodded. He then let slip the few words he couldn't hold in. "It can't be me."

His words rang with the poignancy of someone who would've bitten the bullet himself if he was so able, and Kazuki knew that was the reason. He could feel the fact enter his brain.

"The scar on my eye."

The single scar that had robbed Soshi's eye of sight. It had robbed him of something else as well: the strength to do anything in this situation. Indeed, the right to even obtain such strength. As the knowledge of these incomprehensible facts encircled Kazuki's brain, he felt a strange impact much like the one he had felt when

Soshi called out to him that morning.

Meanwhile, Kazuki was looking into a black ocean. The crashing of the waves once again came to life inside him. He turned his back on the light and began swimming into the cold, expanding darkness. He saw darkness behind Soshi.

"Kazuki. I'm counting on you," Soshi said. Kazuki felt like something was beckoning to him.

His destination was the darkness. The darkness of a freezing black ocean.

At last, the time has come, he thought. The moment of no escape. He couldn't tell if he was happy or sad about it. One more year and he'd be off this island—he could feel that notion sinking into the cold abyss as he spoke.

"Okay," he said, his voice terribly dry.

After breaking away from Soshi and the others, Kuramae and Kazuki ran down the pathway with Kuramae in the lead. They boarded an elevator. As it took them even further into the ground, the two of them remained silent for some time.

"I was adopted," Kuramae said quietly, shortly before the elevator doors reopened.

"Huh? By who?" Kazuki asked by reflex.

"The Minashiro family," she said. "Minashiro-kun's father had been looking after me. Actually, I lived separately, but he did a lot for me. Kind of like the father I never had."

"Kuramae, what about your parents?"

"I don't have any. You don't have a mother either, right?"

"Y-yeah."

"They say there was a big battle when we were kids."

"A battle?"

"That's why a lot of kids on this island don't have fathers or mothers, or either. Did you know that? There are lots of adopted kids besides me."

"You mean like Koyo?"

"Yeah. And Shoko-chan."

"Huh?" Kazuki went blank for a moment. "Shoko, too?"

"Yeah. I'm not sure if she knows, but I'm fairly knowledgeable about these things because I was a test...a test pilot."

"A pilot—" There was something very chilling about that word. Fear, mixed with that same numbing cold that he felt while swimming in the dark ocean of his dream, crept through his arms and legs. "You mean for that thing you mentioned before we came inside? The...'Fafner'?"

"Yes." Kuramae nodded and the elevator doors opened. They exited into a wide open area, where they could see a row of countless cylindrical objects. It was like those train platforms you see on TV sometimes, Kazuki thought. He had lived his whole life on an island that had no trains. Even under these circumstances, he couldn't help but think it was a little cool.

"This is the Bahnzweck. It's how we get around," Kuramae said, and began to head for one of the cylinders. She operated a panel beside the platform, and a part of the cylinder slid open horizontally, making it look all the more like a train.

Kazuki was struck by the notion that, once he entered, there would be no turning back. Conversely, this meant that as of now, he still could. But he didn't. Soshi was counting on him. Soshi believed in him. With that in mind, Kazuki couldn't run away.

He boarded the cylindrical object known as the Bahnzweck. The inside walls were lined with rectangular cushioned seats, just like a train. The outside surface was reflective like a mirror, but you could see through it from the inside.

Kuramae told him to sit, which he did. The doors closed, and he felt a bit of pressure come from his side. Just then, the Bahnzweck was fired. Not just launched; *fired* was the appropriate term for something this fast.

"The ocean—" Looking outside, he was amazed to discover they were in the middle of the ocean. They were shooting through the dark water at an incredible speed. "Wh-what's going on?"

"It's a type of linear car. It runs on magnets. On six wires."

"Wires? You mean like those electric train cables? Cool," he said with a snicker. He noticed that Kuramae was smiling as well.

"You're like a kid," she said. Kazuki realized he was on his knees with his nose pressed against the window as he gazed outside. He had forgotten all about his anxiety and fear in favor of pure excitement.

"Sorry."

He scrambled back to a proper seating position.

"It's okay. Much better than falling into a panic because of pre-deployment nerves or fear."

"Deployment?" Kazuki felt his heart cry out at the word. The thing that had been constantly approaching since before was now right in front of him. His hands grew sweaty. He was all the more thankful that he was surrounded by ocean. The blackness of the surrounding water weakened his desire to run away.

"How aware are you of what you're going to be doing from here?"

"Probably boarding that Fafner thing, right?"

"Well, not exactly 'boarding' it. You'll *become* it. It's not something you pilot. You will enter a state in which you *are* the Fafner."

"I...think I sort of get it."

"Looks like your awareness restriction code level has gone up," Kuramae said with a nod. Kazuki was confused. He still didn't know what to make of that expression. "You've already undergone six hundred hours of hypnotic memorization learning since you were thirteen years old. It was all leading up to one fateful day. That day is today. Furthermore, as far as your inductive learning to stimulate physical training ...well, your grades were top notch."

"Inductive learning?" He hadn't ever heard the term before.

"It's used to manipulate your desire to exercise your body and to learn. So that you can handle, for example, independent physical training fundamentals or real-life conflicts..."

Kazuki was struck by a very unpleasant feeling as he tried to wrap his brain around what she was saying. The boys of this nowhere town had invested infinite amounts of energy into suppressing their ever-present boredom. Hence the Ocean Baseball. Hence Kazuki's unending string of challenges. Hence his constant trouncing of his opponents, one after another.

Inductive? Someone was *making* them exercise? To enhance their physical ability?

He had to stop himself from thinking too deeply about it. After all, they were fun times either way. Maybe that was just desperate thinking.

Kuramae guessed what he was thinking. "But it wasn't like you were being controlled. They simply stimulate your subconscious and encourage learning by grouping it with the idea of fun. It's to provide an optimally effective education. Then, it's just a matter of remembering everything stored in your subconscious, one thing at a time. That's...pretty much all I can tell you. I guess my role is finished." This was exactly the opposite of how Kuramae had been when she lashed out at Soshi.

"But you're a test pilot, right? Why don't *you* get in the Fafner?"

"I'm the one who created the Synergetic Code index."

Kazuki was so lost he almost wanted to apologize. "Cinna-what?"

"In other words, I carried out experiments to clarify the difference between people who can and can't board Fafners. My personal statistics happened to be optimal for those experiments. I even did a little bit of battle training, but my results weren't even fit to be used as standards for a simulation. I...I know that even if did board the unit, I'd only cause it damage."

"I don't really follow you, but ...in other words, I wouldn't have been able to board it either if it weren't for you, right?"

Kuramae looked at him with surprise on her face.

"Am I wrong?"

"No, I...don't think so."

"I get the feeling Soshi's pretty grateful for you."

Kuramae frowned. "I wonder."

"It's just a guess, but maybe he doesn't want you to get inside that thing. Because it's dangerous, I mean. Like maybe the dangerous stuff is where I'm supposed to come in," Kazuki said, not fully sure what his basis for all of this was. It was most likely half spurred by anxiety. Maybe that's all it was for Kazuki—he was just saying comforting things to ease his own nerves.

But that's not all it was to Kuramae.

"Thank you," she said with a smile. Her bladelike demeanor seemed to have vanished. "Are you glad I'm here?"

It was a strange question. It probably wasn't Kazuki, but Soshi, or perhaps Soshi's father that she really wanted to ask. Not just in this moment, but always.

Kazuki felt like he was only using her to dispel his own anxiety, and the guilt began to kick in.

"Yes," he said. It was from the heart. Strangely, he really was glad she was there. He was grateful that she had eased his anxiety by talking with him, but, more than that, maybe he just wanted to answer on behalf of Soshi.

"We're about to arrive." Kuramae rose to her feet and turned her back on him, as if she had spotted the station in the distance. Kazuki realized she was looking in the wrong direction, but said nothing. Somehow he knew that she had only stood up because she didn't want him to see her face.

He also pretended not to hear her sniffling.

She did her best to be inconspicuous as she wiped the corner of her eye.

Just then, something hit the Bahnzweck with incredible force.

With just enough time to remind himself to roll, Kazuki was thrown to the floor. He distributed the shock evenly throughout his body and quickly returned to his feet.

The lights immediately went out. Incredible sparks flashed in the pitch black darkness. The wires outside were touching against the wall of the cylinder, and they were on fire.

Several seconds later, the emergency power kicked in. Dark red lights lit up, but they didn't reach the back end of the vehicle, and it remained pitch black. Kuramae's scream resonated throughout the Bahnzweck.

"Kuramae!" Kazuki shouted as he searched for her. She was nowhere to be found. In a space as confined as this, it was ridiculous. He focused his eyes on the darkness—on the rear of the vehicle—and froze in horror.

The darkness was dragging her in.

"Kuramae!" He began to make his way toward her.

"Stay back!" she screamed, most likely using every ounce of courage she had, struggling to ignore the fact that she wanted him to rescue her. "Get to the front, to the emergency escape room! Cut it off!"

Cut what *off?* he wanted to ask. Could he really do such a thing?

"Hurry!"

He could feel his heart rending inside him. The word *war* pounded inside his head. It wasn't just something edging ever closer. It was something right under his feet.

He began to run from the expanding blob of darkness at the rear of the Bahnzweck and charged towards the front wall. Without thinking anything, he opened up a part of the wall and pushed a lever inside as information automatically popped into his head. A door opened, and he entered the small room that it led to.

He looked back at Kuramae.

"Be careful! The enemy is reading your thoughts for sure!" she screamed, her body completely swallowed in darkness up to the neck. In spite of her own tears, in spite of the fear and the sadness, she continued screaming to the very end, hoping to leave him with something.

There was nothing he could do. His head was swirling with information.

The Wurm Sphere: the enemy's high-level attack which wrenched and distorted space within a sphere. The pitch black ball, known as a distortive rotating object, created superphysical motion, and was, for all intents and purposes, a black hole with a controlled range. Anything it swallowed would become one with the void.

"Thanks f...saying .... glad I was ....re..." Kuramae was crying. Kazuki had witnessed unprecedented courage. The unfathomable courage to express one's thanks to a person when standing at death's doorstep. The pitch black ball of a vortex swallowed her voice and every last tear. Her face was completely engulfed, and her right hand was the last thing to remain struggling, groping at nothing, until it, too, vanished into oblivion.

With a clean sound like something being severed, the black ball evaporated into nothingness. Only a hollowed out sphere of space remained.

Seawater began to flood into it.

Kazuki shouted at the top of his lungs as he shut the door. His body moved without thought. He began operating the emergency controls. It reminded him of the breakfast he had made after waking up that morning. It was nothing more than a routine action he could've done even in his sleep. It was just information that had appeared in his head at some point. It was him, but it wasn't. The real him was just a fear-stricken beast, howling and screaming.

With a sound like *vwoom*, it began to accelerate.

The room he was in was cut off from the rest of the vehicle, almost as if it were trying to escape from the very fact that Kuramae had saved him. The Bahnzweck raced down the remaining track and came to its island destination.

"Are you alive?!"

The hatch opened from the outside.

An adult pulled Kazuki out by the hand, and light struck his face.

"What about Kuramae?" he asked, feeling a sense of incredible self-hatred. An enraged voice welled up inside him. *Like anyone besides you knows the answer to that. What are you doing, trying to weasel out of the blame?* He felt a very real pain, and it was piercing.

The adults, dressed in work fatigues, answered him only with silence and darkened expressions.

Kazuki clenched his teeth and squeezed his voice through them. "Is this where the Fafner...?"

This was more important than asking where he was. He had to get the question out before he started bawling like an infant.

"Yes. We've received orders to have Mark Elf on standby for deployment. We completed the unit check two hours ago. The cockpit block is also ready to go." The adults pulled him to his feet, and then he saw it.

The Dock.

Like a castle made of ultra-hard metal. The entire place was sparklingly polished. The ceiling was as high as a person could look, and it was even wider than the shelter. There was a round control system in the center with a countless number of flashing electronic displays. The walls and ceiling were lined with windows to the monitor room, and the place was filled with more people than Kazuki had ever even seen on the island, all of them busy at work.

They brought him before the thing that had long been awaiting him. He became all the more dominated by the notion that there was no getting out of this now. Even if he tried to make a break for it, the adults would be sure to catch him right away. And then they'd just angrily force him.

It was a bitter truth he understood all too well.

"This is it." Kazuki raised his face too see his speaker. In that instant, it felt like something had passed through his body. It wasn't preparedness or capitulation, but a gentler, more natural emotion. You might say it felt like a reunion.

Something jet-black stood there, locked inside steel framework.

Darkness, Kazuki thought. It was pitch black darkness that had donned the form of a human being and froze that way. It was the cold, dark ocean itself. It was what he had seen behind Soshi. It was the darkness that swallowed Kuramae.

It was so gigantic that looking up at it put a strain on Kazuki's neck. Its limbs somehow suggested the form of a reptile. Each and every curve came together to form a perfectly modeled unit.

"This is ...the Fafner," Kazuki said. It was the first time he had ever seen it, but he just didn't feel that way. And it wasn't just because of the stream of information automatically entering his head. It felt like this was the darkness he had seen when he turned his back on that light. It felt like another Kazuki was standing before him. It was strikingly similar to the shock he had felt when Soshi started talking to him for the first time in five years.

But, things being as they were, he felt no fear. No nervousness either. Just the hot sensation of something forming on the inside of his eyelids that was either caused by joy or sadness, but he couldn't tell which. He cast his eyes downward.

The surrounding adults seemed to be worried that Kazuki might be getting cold feet. "Yes. Fafner. It's the name of the giant who turned into a dragon to protect treasure."

"Those who bathe in the blood of the dragon become immortal. That is what you're going to do."

The adults gave various words of roundabout encouragement, but it was a convenient diversion for Kazuki. It was just like when Kuramae had stood up and hidden her face from him.

He wiped the corner of his eye and looked up. "The Mark Elf," he whispered to internalize the name of his partner—of the steel darkness standing before him.

The cockpit block was a completely separate component from the main body of the Fafner. It was a sort of machine which connected the human to the Fafner. It looked something like a silver egg turned on its side, and rested on an enormous conveyor belt. Kazuki entered through an open hatch to find an incredibly soft seat.

"This is an emergency deployment. You don't have a Synergetic Suit, so this will put some stress on your body. Understand?"

Kazuki nodded silently, even though he didn't understand most of what this person was saying. He was much more concerned with what he would suddenly "remember" next.

The Nibelung System, a voice said inside his mind. Kazuki reflexively reached his hands out for it. At the end of each of the seat's arm rests was a silver, semi-spherical object. Kazuki touched both of them and their covers automatically slid open. Beneath the covers, the objects were filled with bright red gel. Or, at least, that was what it looked like. Buried inside the gel was a row of five metal rings.

They're the Nibelung rings. The new information appeared inside his head. They were the rings that would stimulate his brain's Reptilian complex to the max. They would cleanly erase any feelings of affection or sympathy and turn him into a giant mass of hostility.

Kazuki inserted his hands into the gel on the left and right. It felt extremely warm. He half-expected some of it to spill out, but an electrical solidification process prevented that from happening.

Starting with his right index finger, followed by the thumb, he began inserting his fingers into the rings within the gel. Each of the ten rings wrapped around the base of one of his fingers. Then, they automatically shrank in diameter to fit perfectly, snugly grabbing hold of the fingers as if to never let go of them again.

At that moment, he felt an incredible jolt.

An electric shock traveled up from the base of his fingers, and linking devices attached to the seat rose up and clamped onto his arms, stomach, and legs.

The words *electric chair* came to mind, not as new information, but simply as an expression of pain. His scream reverberated around the cockpit. A moment before the seat had shocked him, the hatch had closed.

He opened his eyes to find himself in a dimly illuminated, sealed space. The pain subsided, leaving him with an incredible sense of relief. It was so cozy, he wondered if he was about to go back to being an infant. The gentle, hypnotic light, the electronic stimulation, and ergonomic design of the vessel lulled him into a sense of peacefulness.

He could feel something beginning to lift up the silver egg with him inside it. Thinking he was about to be inserted into the main body of the Fafner, suddenly the entire vessel tilted forward. It had rotated upside down. His arms and body were completely strapped in, keeping him from falling, but it reminded him all the more of some kind of torturous electric chair. He was hanging upside down. But, just as he was about to scream for them to wait, his body became extremely light.

It felt like up and down had returned to normal. But, in reality, it seemed like his head must've still been pointed toward the ground. It was like he was floating upside down in a body of warm liquid, curled in a ball.

It was the position of a fetus. A voice told him so.

The cockpit block had been inserted into the main body of the Fafner upside down, entering the area between the upper and lower back. A conductive relation between the Fafner and the cockpit then freed the pilot of most of his body's weight, sending him into a fetus-like posture. The Fafner was pregnant with the pilot.

Though his body had become light, he felt a weight in his arms and legs. Or rather, he felt as if they had become heavy. It was proof that his joints had loosened and his nerves had stabilized. Warmth spread from the tips of his hands and feet throughout his body, and he felt great pleasure simply by breathing. He could hear his own heart beating with perfect rhythm. The beating spread throughout his body, creating a sensation similar to the rhythmic crashing of waves.

He got the feeling he knew exactly what would happen if he ever stopped swimming in that dark ocean.

It, in all its vastness, would embrace him.

He would *become* the ocean.

Kazuki closed his eyes. There was deep darkness. He could feel it undulating. It was trying to release a force.

Kazuki knew that preparations were complete. The position of the sun changed, shadows surrounded him, and a different world appeared. Meanwhile, he had arrived exactly where he was supposed to.

Just then...

"Open your eyes, Kazuki." A voice echoed inside his mind.

It wasn't the voice of information implanted within him.

It was the voice of Soshi, from aboard the Siegfried System.

A red phantom image of Soshi appeared in the darkness. Once a pilot had unified with the Fafner, his consciousness would be linked with that of the System operator.

Aha, Kazuki thought at the sight of Soshi's lean face. *So Soshi's in the pit of darkness, just like me.*

It was like they were having a reunion in the middle of a dark ocean at night, after they had both turned their back on the light. These were Kazuki's feelings, but to be sure, they might have half belonged to Soshi as well. They had entered a mutual state in which they shared a single consciousness, as well as some of each other's emotions and memories. They were able to achieve a mutual understanding based on the tiniest fragment of a thought.

It was like he had become Maya Tomi, Kazuki thought. It made him unbelievably happy to know that he too had a sort of telepathic bond with someone.

"Unite with the Fafner and open your eyes. The Fafner's eyes are your eyes."

Kazuki did as told. He fully understood his orders.

Before opening his eyes—though in reality he might as well have—he became aware of his sense of vision.

The Fafner's eyesight function wasn't something that appeared on a monitor; the visual cortex of Kazuki's brain received it directly.

At last, he opened his eyes. Light flooded in, covering an incredibly wide range. It was more than twice as wide as his physical eyes allowed him to see. He could see both the ceiling and the floor of the dock at the same time. He could see diagonally behind himself to the right and left at the same time, as well.

As he experienced the "Goat's Eye View" for the first time, he suddenly knew why it had to be him. Why they had to put a kid in here instead of one of the adults hustling around the dock. The reason was simple: it was impossible for them. Adults wouldn't be able to accept all of this. Only children had minds flexible enough to allow something like this new sense of vision. Really, even many children didn't have that ability.

If even a hint of doubt sparked up suggesting that this thing wasn't him, Kazuki's unity with the Fafner, as well as his shared consciousness with Soshi, would all come crumbling down. But, if that was the case, he was game to go through whatever metamorphosis necessary. If it was a matter of losing a telepathic partner, he was more than willing to acknowledge himself as a jet-black steel beast.

As Kazuki accepted all of this as a reality and new information continued to enter his mind, the cage encompassing him—encompassing the Fafner—began to release. All negative thoughts regarding his inability to run away had already been completely wiped out. It was just as Maya had said this morning. He had woken up to find a different person staring back at him in the mirror. Doors had been opening one-by-one,

unbeknownst to him, and before he knew it he had gone through a complete metamorphosis.

The human Kazuki inside the cockpit block had entered a state equivalent to sleep. Meanwhile, the Fafner Mark Elf had energy surging throughout its entire body, waiting for the moment to exploit its own functionality to its maximum potential—and it, too, was Kazuki.

Soshi's phantom had disappeared from sight as soon as he opened his eyes, but his presence was still clear inside Kazuki's head. Soshi was watching the newly released Kazuki from the inside, guiding him.

"Mark Elf, take the weapon."

He called him not by the name *Kazuki,* but by the number of the unit. It was a way of stabilizing the pilot's psychological sense of unity with the machine.

I am Mark Elf.

Kazuki focused on that one thought as he grabbed the weapon being carried by a crane on his right side.

The Mark Elf is me.

The weapon had a reassuring weight to it, which he felt clearly in his hand.

It was a Ruga Lance. Similar to a jousting lance, it was a monstrous, thirty-six meter-long, electrically charged blade. As he clutched onto it, he also confirmed a stream of information regarding the various weapons stored inside his armor.

Meanwhile, information provided by the System regarding the enemy scrolled through his head. Direction of invasion, number of enemies, confirmed attack patterns—most of it was beyond Kazuki's comprehension at this point, but he would remember what it all meant when the necessity arose.

A siren rang out, and Kazuki was shocked to discover that only seventy minutes had passed. Seventy minutes since Maya had stopped him and Soshi from leaving through the school gate.

Within those seventy minutes, the world had completely transformed, without leaving so much as a trace of its former self.

"As the cage is released, you will proceed to the circuit. The Nightmare Gate will be released in five seconds." Soshi's voice came in as the Mark Elf began to descend. The platform beneath its feet dropped down like an elevator, bringing it to a different area. The ceiling shut above him, and the surrounding area flooded with water. The refreshing touch of water was soothing to his blood-surged body—and to the body of the machine. It was something like a decompression chamber, but this place served another purpose. It wasn't just water, but a liquid which formed a membrane around the Fafner through an electrical process. It was a see-through shock absorbent. It encased the Fafner, and then a door appeared before its eyes.

"Fafner Mark Elf, prepare for deployment!" As soon as Soshi spit out the command, the Fafner was launched out. Kazuki felt an incredible acceleration.

The Mark Elf blasted through a tunnel filled with seawater like a lone bullet. The acceleration made him think of the Bahnzweck. He recalled the image of Kuramae being devoured by that black ball. Kazuki's fear of the enemy—as well as a fuming rage which almost totally eclipsed it—welled up inside him.

I'll make the enemy shed the same tears as Kuramae!

The thought turned him into a mass of vengeance. Violent impulses welled up inside of him to the point that it was almost bizarre. This was thanks to the ten rings stuck on his hands. They didn't just bolster his unity with the Fafner; they also stimulated the mind's most primitive section to its maximum limit.

The Mark Elf blasted through the tunnel into the middle of the sea. It then continued to the surface.

The familiar island coastline suddenly looked smaller than it ever had before. His heart filled with joy and superiority at the thought of how enormous he had become. He touched down on the rocky soil, shaking the earth beneath him. The shock absorbent encasing his body returned to its liquid form and splashed and shimmered all around him.

"Move out immediately, Mark Elf." Soshi's words reached Kazuki more quickly than his voice. Kazuki—the Mark Elf—charged forth, wielding its enormous blade. Most of the adults on the island must have been watching the deployed Mark Elf like it was some kind of god. They must have been cheering in awe at the sight of this steel giant running at such incredible speeds. Such were Soshi's thoughts, and Kazuki shared them.

The two of us have become one, to annihilate the enemy. We'll do what the adults couldn't.

The western coastline was in a dreadful state.

Everywhere, it had been hollowed out by spheres, leaving the dead fragments of buildings and tanks strewn about.

Kazuki raced through an area saturated with smoke and came to a hill, where he saw something taking root at the top. The enemy had spread roots into the ground and was trying to bore into the island. It was like a gigantic, shining golden tree, breathing gracefully. Kazuki saw that its roots flashed with the colors of the rainbow, and the surrounding earth transformed to match it.

The enemy's trying to assimilate the whole island?

Kazuki and Soshi shared this realization.

This is the thing that killed Kuramae.

Soshi shared Kazuki's lust for vengeance.

Likewise, Kazuki shared Soshi's understanding of the enemy.

"Festum."

The collective term for the enemy. This particular enemy was a Sphinx model, so named because it was the presenter of the enemy's message—its question—which had begun their worldwide invasion.

"Question." A clear voice.

For a split second, an image of the silver radio flashed in Kazuki's mind. Two and a half seconds had passed since deployment. Two beings were present.

The Fafner, Mark Elf.

The Sphinx model Festum.

They were the two beings that would complicate Kazuki's world, shattering it to pieces so that it could never be reassembled.

In response to the approaching Mark Elf, the enemy's glowing grew immediately more intense.

"Are you—"

A gentle voice came through, as if stroking his very heart.

"Are you there?"

Prickle. The voice traveled right through the Mark Elf's thick armor into the cockpit block, giving Kazuki goosebumps all over.

He felt the voice shake his very existence. And then, a sense of understanding came over him. The very consciousness which affirmed his existence—the being who embraced a human sense of self-awareness—*that* was the Festum's enemy.

He knew what the enemy was really asking: "Are you a living, thinking creature, or are you like a stone dropped in there?"

It seemed as though it was saying, "If you *are* a living, thinking creature, I'll turn you into a stone."

Once again, the children's silver radio came to mind.

The children, gathered around it with pricked ears, waiting for a "voice" to come through.

The uncertainty of what would happen if they answered it.

Seven years later—

Kazuki was there. The Kazuki who had turned his back to the light. Who had become one with the dark ocean. Who had unified with this hunk of jet-black steel. He was there, and he sent out an answer to the "question." Not with words or even thoughts, but through a much simpler action.

He lifted the thirty-six meter-long, ultra-heated blade and, using the momentum from his dash for extra power, severed the roots the enemy was trying to use to dig its way into the ground with a single slash. The severed roots writhed and wriggled, emitting a blinding light.

The main body of the enemy proceeded to move to the side in midair, in an attempt to escape Kazuki's attack range.

Wait a minute. Hey!

Thanks to his "Goat's Eye View", he could clearly track the enemy's movements.

Come here.

He could've sworn it was laughing at him.

I'll drag your sparkling ass into this darkness.

Quivering with the impulse to destroy his enemy, he swung his lance. Blue-white sparks flew everywhere. Just before reaching the enemy, the blade struck an invisible wall and was deflected. The enemy had deployed a high-level defensive barrier that could easily repel collisions with physical objects or redirect their path. There was only one way to destroy it.

"Stay sharp! Advance, Mark Elf!" Soshi screamed.

Kazuki screamed as well, but there were no words. He made contact with the enemy's barrier, starting with the left shoulder. Entering the Assimilation Mode, he suddenly broke through.

Kazuki felt very clearly that he had entered it.

The next moment, his jet-black steel began to take on a golden glow.

"Are you—"

The voice pounded inside his mind. The last part of the sentence came not in the form of words, but as a golden glow, so intense as to stain one's very soul.

It was the instant immediately before Assimilation.

The right half of the enemy's body began to change shape, sprouting seven breathtakingly beautiful wings. The rainbow-colored, crystalline slats that formed them stretched out, one after another, and began to wrap around the left half of the Mark Elf.

Kazuki was assaulted by an overwhelmingly intense shimmer, a sense of calmness, and a desire to submit.

"Kazuki!!" Soshi screamed in desperation.

"Yeah, yeah, I know," Kazuki responded via thought rather than words. He had already turned his back on the light long ago. No matter how beautiful this glimmering being before him may have been, he had chosen the darkness.

With bitter conviction, Kazuki swung his blade. The thirty-six meter-long super-heated lance tore through the shining wings, slicing off more than half of them in a single stroke.

Perhaps the enemy felt betrayed. The remaining rings suddenly sharpened to points and swung down towards the Mark Elf's shoulder and belly. Kazuki dodged with uncanny reflexes.

The jet-black machine ducked with the speed of

a shadow. An enormous blade swung past its head. The armor on its left shoulder and upper leg took the rest. The armor cracked, and the blades sunk in. The damage reached Kazuki's consciousness in the form of pain. But it was hardly enough to dampen his fighting spirit.

He quickly stuck the tip of his blade into the left side of the enemy's belly. He felt immense pleasure in his ability to so easily manipulate what would have otherwise been an incredibly unwieldy weapon. Continuing to act in accordance with the automatic stream of information, he flicked a trigger on the weapon, and the blade—still stuck inside the enemy—split down the middle. It opened to the left and right, widening the enemy's wound. Then it fired a shot.

The open blade had become the barrel of a super-conductive gun, and from it launched a two hundred-ten kilogram bullet. A super-high voltage shock fired out as the enemy was nailed with a multi-kiloton blast.

The enemy's lower belly blew apart into a mangled mass, sending glittering, rainbow-colored fragments everywhere. But the enemy didn't stop. That wasn't nearly enough damage to defeat it.

On the contrary, its shimmering only grew more intense. More than twice as many wings as before sprouted from its left side. There would be no dodging it this time. Kazuki made a quick judgment and released his right hand from the blade, then held it up to shield himself.

He was struck with blazing pain as the enemy pierced through his right arm, shoulder, side, and leg. Unlike anything he had ever felt before, the pain began to break down his will to fight. The agonizing feeling of his own flesh being destroyed gave way to the realization that this was in fact just a machine, not his own flesh. That was a worst-case scenario. If he couldn't go on believing that this destroyed unit was himself, his unity with it would be sent into discord.

Kazuki flew into a rage. It wasn't just that he had taken damage; it was that the enemy had *caused* him to take damage. Injury bred revenge. Kill or be killed. If you get nailed, nail them back. It was as simple as that.

Kazuki twisted his body with a countless number of enemy blades still embedded in the arms and legs. It was extremely painful, but that was just kindling for the raging fire inside him.

He took the lance back and returned it to its original position, then used it to slice off the blades in his arm and leg. Now was the chance to free himself—but his right arm was useless.

The enemy's wings transformed into tentacles, wrapping around the Mark Elf's arm several times over. They began to enter the unit through the holes of its wounds and commence a piece-by-piece Assimilation.

It was horrifying; the pain had vanished from what should have been a badly wounded arm. Moreover, some sort of miraculously soothing sensation was coming from his wounds. There was a sense of calmness several times stronger than what he felt upon boarding the Fafner. It aroused a desire for peace. It was making him want to just entrust his soul to this glowing light before him.

So this was the enemy's tactic, he thought.

Wound the target, and then take away his pain. This would take the edge off the target's willpower.

In a very fundamental way, Kazuki felt that the very fact that the enemy had wounded him was an insult. The enemy was mocking his pain, violating his human dignity, and this caused Kazuki to explode with rage.

Don't fuck with me! If you've got the nerve to start healing me, here's how it's gonna be!

Kazuki swung down the blade in his left hand, delivering through it all of his rage and hatred.

The sensation of his right arm being severed at the elbow shot straight to his brain. Enduring a nauseating, dizzying pain, Kazuki took back his freedom. His heart swelled with gloating joy.

Stratified liquid mercury sprayed from his half-severed arm like blue blood.

"Activating Pain Block in the right arm region." The blood stopped as Soshi's voice came in. The sliced tip of the elbow broke apart even more and detached. The cells eroded away at an alarming rate, forfeiting the arm's functionality, but, as a result, Kazuki could feel the pain fade away.

By that time, he was already brandishing his blade again. An instant before plunging the ultra-heated tip of it into the enemy's chest, he sensed the enemy's confusion. Of course, it wasn't that he could read the enemy's thoughts. After all, the enemy was non-human for sure, and unlike any living creature Kazuki had ever seen before.

But somehow, in that single moment, he could tell. "Why," the enemy was thinking. "Why couldn't I read your mind?"

So that was his trick, Kazuki thought. The enemy read people's thoughts. It would enter your mind and figure out what action you were going to take before you took it. Kazuki understood that this was definitely the enemy's most fearsome ability, and he was glad.

By remaining unified with the Fafner and activating the Assimilation Mode, Kazuki had completely intercepted the enemy's dreadfully corrosive ability. His mind was out of the enemy's reach. There was an outstanding sense of superiority in that. On the battlefield, there was utter joy in being able to deprive the enemy of their most desired thing and deliver one-way beatings in its place.

The tip of his blade sunk into the enemy's chest. It would then proceed to drive a bullet like the previous one directly into the enemy's heart—into its true being.

In the meantime, however, the enemy attempted several forms of resistance.

First, it attempted to prevent the blade from opening up to widen the wound by wrapping its tentacles around it. There was a fierce clash for a moment, but the blade ultimately opened after Kazuki rapidly flicked the handle trigger several times.

Immediately following this, the enemy reactivated its high-level defensive barrier. The Mark Elf struck the invisible wall so hard that even the enemy's frame dented. The Fafner's armor twisted and caved in, the skeleton squealed, and there was a pain so excruciating Kazuki wondered if his shoulder had been dislocated.

But pain only served to bolster his unity with the Mark Elf. Pain was the dragon's blood; those who bathed in it were immortal. The words he was told before deployment rose once again in his mind. He finally understood their meaning. They were referring to the Fafner itself. Right now, Kazuki could foil every single ace up the enemy's sleeve. He had awakened the Reptilian Complex in his mind. The Fafner had made him an unkillable hero.

There stood the Mark Elf, undestroyed. It wasn't even knocked off balance. It burst through the enemy's barrier via a perfectly executed transition into Assimilate Mode, and readied its finger on the bullet-firing trigger.

Suddenly, he saw something appear in the enemy's chest.

An enormous human face.

Kazuki stared at its sullen, teary-eyed expression.

The face belonged to Kuramae.

Are you glad I'm here?

A voice resonated—or so he thought. The enemy hadn't spoken; it had opened a hole in order to penetrate Kazuki's mind, and, in that instant, Kazuki processed the hole as a voice.

At the same time, Kazuki learned what had happened to Kuramae. Her will to exist crushed, her screams echoed in his head ceaselessly. But it wasn't Kuramae. Kuramae was no more. She had been wiped out by the golden, godlike enemy—assimilated.

The thing before his eyes was merely a reconstruction of information the enemy had obtained through Kuramae. It was something resembling Kuramae's face, but not her face.

This realization didn't come in fast enough to protect Kazuki's mind.

As Kuramae's voice continued, the enemy's power swept over him. Soshi was yelling something, but it was hard to make out.

It entered...

...his mind.

Kazuki's desire to defeat this enemy suddenly vanished. In the blink of an eye, the enemy slipped in even deeper.

"Are you—"

The enemy gently stroked the inside of his heart.

"Are you there?"

Kazuki's eyesight quickly began to go black. He searched for the light in a daze, only to find that a completely different image had appeared.

He thought he saw someone.

It was himself.

Suddenly, he felt like he had shrunk. His enormous presence had contracted to its original helpless state in one fell swoop.

No, it was someone even more helpless than him—it was himself as a child.

At some point, the voice resonating in his head had turned into a sea of crickets chirping.

The suffocating scent of greenery.

Summer. Kazuki was in a grove by the grounds of a shrine on the eastern part of the island. In his left hand, he held a weapon. Or rather, a tree branch that had *become* his weapon. It was exactly the same length as young Kazuki's arm, and he stood there gripping onto it, frozen in place.

He noticed that the tip of it was wet.

The unchangeable crimson of the wetted tip leapt to his vision.

"It hurts! It hurts!" An incredible scream rose up. Unprecedented terror pierced through Kazuki's heart.

"Ah..." He whimpered in fear as he looked at the other person present.

There was one other child there at that time, and the sight of him terrified Kazuki.

Two children in a muggy summer's grove.

One was Kazuki Makabe.

The other was Soshi Minashiro.

Soshi, cowering on the ground, pressing his hand to the left side of his face, crying out in pain. His jaw, cheek, and nose were wet with blood that spilled through the cracks in his hand and glinted in the sun.

Staring at Soshi as he sobbed and hollered, Kazuki wondered why.

Why was there a tree branch in his hand? Why was Soshi's hand dark red? Why?

Maybe it was some kind of game. Maybe it was just an impulse that had come over him. Maybe he had no particular intentions. Otherwise, maybe Soshi had said something that made him *really* angry. But, even in that case, it would have just been an impulse. Otherwise Kazuki wouldn't have done something like this. He didn't mean to. He had no—

He had no intention of hurting Soshi so deeply. He had to tell him. He had to get him to understand. It was all Kazuki could think about. His wounded friend was screaming right before his eyes, but Kazuki could only think about himself.

"Uwa—"

But the only thing he could get out of his mouth was a voice so cowardly even he was disgusted.

Soshi's remaining right eye, wet with tears, looked back at Kazuki.

Slowly, the hand covering the left side of his face began to open.

"Kazu...ki."

Just after Soshi uttered his name, Kazuki fled.

Screaming all the while, he turned his back on Soshi and desperately ran away. He was just scared. Just thinking about what he had done filled him with fear. Unable to bear it, he ran away. Just as he had done when Kuramae was devoured by the black sphere. He just screamed and ran as hard as he could, straight ahead, back to a safe place.

He ran all the way home and locked himself in his room. Quivering with fear, he waited for time to pass.

But the real terror had only just begun.

Kazuki just sat in silence, waiting for someone to come and accuse him. He waited for the adults to show up, divulging the gritty details of his act and demanding apology and repentance.

But no one ever accused him. His father came home in the evening and wondered if Kazuki had caught a cold. He tried to bring him to the Tomi Hospital, but Kazuki belligerently asserted that it wasn't a cold and prepared to face his father's wrath. But his father didn't get angry. He didn't even seem to have a reason to.

The next day, Kazuki went to school with a frozen numbness traveling throughout his entire body. He imagined himself apologizing before the entire student body. He thought time and again about turning back and running away, but ultimately did not. If he ran now, he would go mad worrying about when his time would come. He would much rather just have someone—*anyone*—take out their anger on him, however harsh it may have been.

But no one was angry. No one accused him and no one demanded an apology. The teachers said nothing—only that Soshi had taken the day off from school.

And the next day as well. And the day after that. Soshi didn't come to school. But not a single person accused Kazuki. The more he thought about what he had done, the more terrified he became.

After a whole week had passed, it finally dawned on him that Soshi hadn't told anyone about where they were that day. He had stayed silent about the fact that Kazuki was standing right beside him the day he was wounded. That was the only explanation. Kazuki's presence had remained unspoken. This realization birthed two sensations within him: unprecedented relief, and guilt. The two churned ceaselessly inside him for days, welling up in the pit of his stomach.

Soshi didn't come to school for two weeks. During that time, Kazuki tried countless times to visit him, to see what had become of him. To learn the extent of the wounds he had inflicted.

But he was too afflicted with fear; he just couldn't go through with it. Instead, he sat and obsessively awaited Soshi's return to school. Perhaps once Soshi turned up, all of Kazuki's sins would be brought into the light of day for everyone on the island to see.

And so a mere two-week period was to become more than enough time to change everything, and to create a rift between Kazuki and Soshi.

Soshi returned to school with his usual smile and his left eye wrapped in bandages. What happened that morning was something Kazuki would never forget, even now. Soshi turned to an awe-struck Kazuki and said one thing:

"Good morning, Kazuki."

Nothing more. Only that altogether too ordinary greeting.

"I fell down on my own," Soshi explained to his concerned friends, leaving a dumbfounded Kazuki in the dust. He offered them a comforting smile. It was a little hard to see, but as long as everyone was willing to help him out, it was no big deal, he said so that Kazuki could hear as well.

No one accused Kazuki. It seemed that the opportunity was gone forever.

Half a year later, Kazuki and Soshi were placed in different classes, and gradually they drifted apart. It was the result of too many irreversible things.

The face of young Soshi screaming out in pain and the face of Soshi wrapped in bandages, smiling gently, popped into Kazuki's mind with shocking clarity. In five years, he had never recalled these things so vividly. They transcended recollection, constantly occupying a corner of his mind.

Why didn't Soshi point the finger? The more Kazuki thought about it, the more he realized he had become a prisoner to the silence. All he had to do was confess, say that he was the one who did it. His inability to do so had locked him in a cell. It was the beginning of a five-year prison sentence, during which silent accusations loomed over him every second of every day.

Wasn't it about time to end it?

So whispered whatever it was that had crept into his heart.

Kazuki felt himself being engulfed in a great calm. The sweet sensation of the enemy controlling him from the inside, trying to devour him.

Mere seconds had passed since it first entered his mind. This was when the rings at last unleashed their true power.

It was the cumulative result of all their research on how to defeat the enemy and the reason the Fafner was to become such a formidable opponent. A function which blocked out all independent thought: the Impulse Vent.

The rings sent such a jolt to a section of Kazuki's psyche—the section directly coupled with those pitch black, violent impulses that had thoroughly evaded the calm—that sparks seemed to be flying inside his brain. It reminded him of how he had endured those five years.

He was fine.

It was hardly enough to move him. In reality, someone being hurt, or the act of hurting someone, was no big deal. Whether the person's scars were big or small, it made no difference to him or anybody else. There was little difference between hurting someone and being hurt, nor was there any logic to it. It was just a common occurrence in the world that may or may not happen at any given time.

If someone was about to hurt you, hurting them back with an equal or greater force was the appropriate thing to do. If someone challenged you with a display of strength, you should respond with the same strength.

Humans were the same as objects. Sometimes they broke. Either they broke down all of a sudden, or they were intentionally destroyed. The difference between the two was minute. There was nothing to be afraid of.

And thus it was by thinking that everything was fine that Kazuki discovered he could endure the situation. In time, he even grew desensitized to the fact that he had become so apathetic. The entirety of his being had wholly absorbed the churning mixture of relief and guilt, leaving not so much as a trace.

Instead, however, he occasionally got the feeling that someone like him ought to just disappear. He was terribly matter-of-fact about it. He had entered a mindset in which it was only natural to turn his back on whatever light might appear. It was a mindset that accepted his prison of eternally damning silence every single day.

Whether he was receiving scars or giving them, it didn't matter to Kazuki.

These were the thoughts that successfully deflected the enemy's relentless psychological invasion.

There was a face before Kazuki's eyes. It was golden and sparkling, and looked like the crying face of Kuramae.

"Kazuki! Don't lose your head!" Soshi's encouragement popped up in his mind. He had forgotten to address him as "Mark Elf." Kazuki was in such a trance that he had to be reminded of who he was.

"Destroy the enemy's core!"

I'm on it, Kazuki responded mentally without bothering to vocalize it. Before Soshi even had time to process that Kazuki had been revived, he clutched the handle of his lance and pulled the trigger.

But the enemy must have been as thankful for those few precious seconds Kazuki had been entranced. In the meantime, it had stuck a tentacle in the gap in the open blade. With an incredible blast, the blade of the Ruga Lance wrenched apart.

Before the enemy's tentacles could lunge together at Kazuki, his left hand reached for his upper thigh. The armor covering his leg opened up, and he grabbed the handgun stored inside.

Wielding it as the symbol of power that it was, he pointed it directly at Kuramae's crying visage and fired. An energy bullet discharged with the force of a tank shell and landed a direct hit, blasting into Kuramae's left eye with an incredible noise.

This was his chance.

His heart filling with rage, he fired a continuous barrage. In less than three seconds he fired off sixteen shots, turning Kuramae's face into a mangled mess. Hot, uncontainable ecstasy ran through him as if his blood had filled with acid.

There's no big difference between hurting and being hurt. It's not a matter of logic. It's just kill or be killed.

And now it's time to show you.

Here's how I've come to regard myself and everyone else over the last five years.

The gunfire ceased for an instant, and the enemy used this window of opportunity to spread its tentacles and lunge at Kazuki in an attempt to tear him limb from limb. For the enemy, resorting to a physical attack like that was fairly low-level. It seemed like a desperate attempt to protect itself from the impending disaster.

For Kazuki, as long as he could operate as necessary, he cared little what the enemy tried to do to his body. He focused solely on the tentacles capable of inflicting lethal damage, beating them away with his damaged right arm. They were the tentacles that had transformed into sharpened blades through the release of high-magnetic pressure. His armor buckled on contact with them and a pain like ice seeped inside, but what did it matter?

As other tentacles cut through his arms, legs, and chest, he tossed aside the handgun and replaced it with yet another weapon. It was a mine blade stored inside the armor on his left arm. He flicked his wrist once to expose the handle of the weapon and clutched onto it. And then, he plunged what would thereafter be his weapon of choice into the chest of his enemy and snapped it.

After a brief moment, the blade-shaped bomb exploded. The right half of Kuramae's face became grotesquely distorted. As soon as he saw it, Kazuki gushed with emotion at the thought that he had done this.

A new blade automatically popped out of the handle. He plunged it into the enemy right next to its open wound. He sunk it in even deeper than the last one and snapped off the handle once again. Before it even exploded, another blade popped out, and he plunged this one in as well.

He stabbed the enemy over and over, mangling it. It had mangled him as well, tearing off pieces of his body, to which Kazuki responded by plunging his blade into its chest.

It was me! It was me! It was me! It was me!

His brain screamed.

I fucked up Soshi's eye! I fucked up Soshi's eye! I did it! Just like this! Like this! Like this! And I'll do the same to you! I'll do it to you! You! It feels good! It feels good! Ah! It's so good!

The rings wrapped around his ten fingers stimulated his most primitive, violent impulses. He converted these impulses into actions without even a hint of reservation and, upon seeing their results, repeated the same actions again and again.

He had torn and blasted Kuramae's face to smithereens. The next thing he knew, the enemy's entire body was covered in a countless number of enormous, unfamiliar faces. He knew they belonged to the people of this island who had been assimilated in battle.

Why was the enemy showing him this? Kazuki wondered. Did it think he would forfeit the ecstasy of destroying it just because a bunch of sad faces were staring at him?

With all twelve mine blades used up, he tossed away the handle and thrust his left hand into the deep, hollowed out wound hole. Inside it sparkled something of true beauty.

The enemy's core. He was so eager to see the bright red kernel of life that he paid no mind to the enemy's frantically lashing tentacles as he tore it out. It was exposed. If he damaged it, the enemy would never recover, and the pleasurable sensation of holding such a thing in the palm of his hand shot up his back to the very tip of his head.

Ah! Ah! Ah! This feels good!

His emotions turned grim as he crushed it in his hand.

The bright red jewel burst, spraying countless flecks of glitter dust. As he gazed at it, he was struck with such incredible ecstasy that Kazuki's body deep within the cockpit block began spasming.

Without wasting any time, something began to

happen to the remains of the beautifully smashed core. What were once miniscule grains had, in an instant, swelled up to create a pitch black orb. A distortive rotational body had formed right in front of him. The black vortex of nothingness swallowed up the Mark Elf before it had a chance to escape. As it tried to erase his existence, Kazuki sensed the Festum presenting its final question.

Is this the outcome of your existence?

A void with no remains. The culmination of a spirit he had obtained through five years of endurance. Just as Kazuki's sense of pleasure began to fade, he saw a darkness like he had never seen before.

He burst into laughter. It was honest, joyful laughter.

You think I'm afraid of disappearing?! Kazuki responded to the enemy with glee.

The black vortex engulfed him and disappeared with a zap.

Hollowed out by the sphere, the soil beneath the ground lay bare.

The Mark Elf was there with all of its armor melted away like hard candy.

Due to the heat created by the distortion of space, some parts of the armor had even evaporated. Nevertheless, the Mark Elf stood tall, its existence still intact. The Assimilation Mode had offset the enemy's power to the very end. Kazuki remained alive deep within the machine's abdomen.

Deep within, where it creaked and grated.

"Uhhh..." he groaned, unable to muster any more of a voice. He felt like the pain was going to drive him mad. The pain in his fingertips was especially excruciating. It felt like all his fingers on both hands had been smashed to pieces and had their nails torn off. All over his body, the pain was so intense that he thought the slightest quiver might make him pass out. And yet, he couldn't stop convulsively screaming in agony. Before he knew it his face was drenched with tears.

"Your unit's damage is tremendous. I'm going to blank your consciousness, Kazuki," Soshi's voice gently resonated in his head. "You did well...Kazuki. You've annihilated the enemy. The pain is too severe. You'd best sleep now."

Kazuki shook his head in shock.

He had been seen, he thought. Soshi had seen all of his ugliness. His weakness as he ran away. His dark impulses, accumulated through a life of pretending he was fine. He had always wanted to apologize for scarring him. He was just so petrified by the deepness of the scar that he couldn't bring himself to apologize or confess to anyone.

That is, with the exception of one person: Maya. She was the one person he had confessed his crime to in five years. But he knew it wouldn't change anything when he confessed. Neither his relationship with Soshi nor the state of his own heart would return to normal.

There was nothing he could do besides cast himself into some dark place.

Kazuki felt himself in an even darker, deeper

ocean than usual. It wasn't his ocean. Soshi had slightly widened the extent to which he shared his consciousness. Kazuki saw the inside of Soshi's heart—a heart probably no other person had seen.

It was a heart filled with unfathomable darkness. Bogged down by a forlorn acceptance of death, he had a deep understanding of the truth. Kazuki wondered just what kinds of things Soshi had seen by now.

Everyone knew that Soshi's father occasionally made him go to places outside the island. It seemed these dark thoughts inside him were due to that. Surely he had seen things with that right eye that Kazuki knew nothing about.

Daringly, he now showed his darkened heart to Kazuki. To comfort him. To show him he wasn't the only one with an ugly heart.

"Thank you," he said abruptly. "Thanks for being there."

Kazuki couldn't respond to these words. He didn't need to.

Before breaking into genuine tears, Soshi guided Kazuki from the System and blanked his consciousness. It was as if he were there, gently supporting the weight of Kazuki's tired body.

There was nothing left to hide. Neither of them had to turn their back on the other as Kuramae had done in the Bahnzweck.

Before his vision went black, Kazuki stared into the painfully blue sky. The enemy had vanished, returning the sky to its usual clear blue. Looking up at it, Kazuki wished with that he could disappear into nothingness. But then, there was a small corner of his anguish-ravaged heart that thought,

But I'm here.

With that, his consciousness fell into the calming lull of oblivion.

Chapter Three
The Days That Come In Due Time

Chapter Three
The Days That Come In Due Time

When Kazuki came to, he found himself in a quiet room crammed with ridiculously large machinery. After a brief interval, he realized that the machinery was arranged around him in his bed. He felt strangely refreshed, as if he had slept deeply without even dreaming.

He quickly sat up in bed.

Various people in white gowns approached him, surprising him a bit. They must have been doctors. One of them looked familiar. It was the doctor from the Western Slope's pride and joy, the Tomi Hospital.

"That's why you're our number one pilot candidate. I'd expect no less from Makabe-san's son. Your recuperative strength is outstanding," Maya's mother said as if lavishing compliments upon her own child.

"Y-yeah."

"You fought well. Thank you so much. The fact that we're all here right now in a safe place and able to talk to one another is thanks to you, Kazuki-kun." She spoke with a sweet voice, telling of just how valuable his execution of the mission had been. Her sincerity embarrassed him quite a bit.

"Um...What happened to my clothes?" Kazuki asked, realizing that he was dressed like a patient. He was afraid he would have to go home dressed like this.

"They're here. Don't worry," she said with clairvoyance befitting of Maya's mother. She pointed to a bin beside the bed. "You can sleep some more if you'd like."

"Is this...Alvis?"

"Yes. It's the Medical Room," she answered. Kazuki suddenly felt horribly uncomfortable.

"I'm...going home."

"Oh? Then a staff member will take you back."

"No, I can go alone."

As he got out of bed, various parts of his body started hurting. Moreover, there were various cords wrapped around his body. Tomi-sensei politely removed them. She had a nice scent. Kazuki became a little jealous of Tomi for having a mother.

He changed his clothes behind a curtain divider.

"If you start getting headaches or nausea or feel strange, tell your father right away, okay?"

Kazuki responded to her gentle words with a firm bow, and left the room.

As he walked, his body felt light and floaty, yet he also felt pain. So this is what they call "muscle pain," he thought as if he had discovered something rare. He put some strength into his wobbly, stumbling body and continued down a hallway lined with Medical Rooms.

"Alvis," Kazuki uttered without even thinking,

and felt a slight shock. He wanted to hurry back to someplace familiar. His own town. His own house. His own room. And here he was, hoping to leave the island in another year. Now that he had really come to an unfamiliar place, he was utterly restless. Once again, he felt like he had discovered something rare.

Going out the door at the end of the hallway, he came to a waiting room. There was a sofa, a decorative plant, and a drink vending machine, as well as a great number of people sitting, wandering around, talking, yelling, and crying.

"You're awake, Kazuki," someone said. Kazuki snapped up straight.

It was Soshi. He stood up from the sofa and lightly stretched both legs. It looked like he had been there waiting for Kazuki the whole time.

"You're wearing your own clothes. Does that mean you're going home?"

Kazuki nodded silently. Soshi spoke in a very natural manner, as if they had been good friends for years. Even though they hadn't had a real conversation in quite some time.

"I'll take you back. There's probably a lot you want to talk about, right?" Soshi said. In reality, he didn't seem to mind whether Kazuki had much to talk about or not.

They exited the waiting room together and got into an elevator. They proceeded through the tunnel, climbed a staircase, and exited Alvis. The exit led to the side of a road on the coastline of the southern part of town. They emerged to see the sun setting in the sky.

"It was just morning," Kazuki blurted out. It was as if an entire day had just vanished. It had been swallowed up by an unknown entity, never to return again.

Kazuki's entire body ached, and he couldn't muster any more strength. His feet grew unsteady, inciting a sense of apprehension.

"Let's rest a bit," Soshi said. He went ahead and took a seat on a concrete bench by the coastline. Kazuki decided to do likewise, and timidly took a seat next to him.

They watched the sun set over the sea. Kazuki realized the evening sun wasn't in its usual place.

"Hey, isn't that...?" He half rose from the bench.

"It's because the camouflage mirror is still down. The position of the sun is backwards."

Soshi's matter-of-fact explanation somehow seemed to drain the power out of Kazuki, and he sat back down.

"You mean west and east were really backwards?"

"North and south, too. They inverted the light coming in from outside, in order to completely hide the island."

Suddenly Ocean Baseball came to Kazuki's mind, before he even had a chance to wonder why they would need to do something like hide the island. If east, west, north, and south were all switched, what were they supposed to call the Eastern Slope and Western Slope teams from now on?

"Wow, it feels like a completely different town now, even though the only thing that's changed is the directions," he said. It was the first time he had expressed a personal opinion to Soshi in quite awhile.

"Not just the directions—the calendar's changed as well," Soshi said.

"The calendar?"

"What month do you think it is?"

"Isn't it April?"

"It's the end of September."

"Huh?"

"Right now, this island is in the Southern Hemisphere. The seasons are reversed."

Kazuki went blank. "Why is it in the Southern...?"

"Tatsumiya Island is a fortified city. It can travel the ocean at up to sixty knots."

"The island...travels? Why aren't we with Japan?"

"Japan was wiped out," Soshi said softly.

"Wiped out? You were just in Tokyo this spring bre—"

"All that's left of Tokyo is deep within the ocean. Eighty percent of the Japanese archipelago was demolished. By the powers of the enemy and of mankind."

"Did you...see it?"

"I did." The brevity of his response spoke volumes of the terror he must have seen. "All the countries of the world have perished. For the last thirty years, the world has been at war, but somehow this island has managed to preserve its peace. Until today, that is."

The word *peace* felt like it was echoing from a very distant place.

"Many of mankind's survivors have worked for a long time on the development of ways to resist the Festum," Soshi continued. "This island is one of them. The plans are only seventy percent finished, but we had to go ahead and jump into combat."

Kazuki still didn't know the real reason for this.

That voice on the silver radio when they were kids.

From that day, the enemy began calculating the possibility of the existence of Tatsumiya Island, until the first unit finally showed up today.

Kazuki still knew nothing of these facts. He just listened to Soshi, trying to accept the reality before his eyes. He knew that was what Soshi wanted him to do.

The world had flipped. It must have been in that instant when the sun changed positions and the shadows streaked across at incredible speed, he thought. That was the moment that had tossed him into an unforeseen future.

"At war..." he whispered, as if to confirm that it was a reality. "Festum..." The name of the enemy. The realization that he had already destroyed one of them gradually welled up inside him.

"That's right. They launched a worldwide invasion that's been expanding ever since. The coming of the Sphinx model means they've definitely detected us. There'll be an all-out invasion sooner or later."

"Those things are coming back?"

"Yeah. For sure. And they'll be a lot more powerful next time. The adults are trying to move the island again and trick them before that happens, but...they won't make it. It'll end up being a matter of escaping the battle zone as we undergo several invasions."

There was a certain absoluteness in the way he spoke. Kazuki realized it was probably the darkness within Soshi that made him talk that way.

"I'm going to get back in...the Fafner, I mean," Kazuki said, as if remembering what he was supposed to do.

"Yeah. But it won't just be you. There are twelve Fafners in all. They're designed to work in cooperation with one another. They'll be selecting the pilot candidates soon, based on who shows signs of Savant Syndrome."

"Sava...?" Kazuki had heard that somewhere before. It didn't take much raking through his memory to figure out where. It was what Soshi had said to Maya when they were trying to leave through the school gate together. "What is that syndrome thing anyway?"

Soshi looked up at him as if to say, "Oh, you don't know?".

"I guess your awareness restriction code hasn't raised that much yet," he snickered for some reason.

"Uh, yeah..." Kazuki said with a confused look. From Soshi's point of view, it was as if someone had finally come to his side of the fence. He was so full of joy that he couldn't help but get ahead of himself. Of course, Kazuki had yet to realize this.

"*Savant* means a genius."

"A genius?"

"Yeah, you could also call it 'Genius Syndrome.' It refers to people who, through whatever combination of special factors, have developed some ability that far surpasses the norm. In Tomi's case, she's developed abnormally sharp observation skills. Her ability lies in dividing things into classifications and drawing connections. If things hadn't changed, she probably could've become a brilliant psychologist or a philosopher, or maybe a religious guru."

"Tomi, a guru?" It was a bizarre notion that Kazuki couldn't imagine. And yet he could. Though something a little more scholarly was probably more suitable. "Do you know what Tomi's hobby is?"

His train of thought interrupted, Soshi stared at him vacantly. "Hobby? No..."

"She's into rock climbing."

"She's a climber?" Evidently a bit surprised by the answer, his eyes perked up. Kazuki gave a nod.

"And she doesn't use a safety rope. She goes up Mount Alone."

Soshi was astounded. Mount Alone was the tallest mountain on Tatsumiya Island, so named because it was too dangerous to visit alone.

"*That's* where she goes climbing? What's she thinking? If she fell she would die."

"Yeah, that's what I said, too."

Kazuki had seen Maya climb rocks a number of times. She always made it look so easy as she just shot up the side of the cliff. She was like a butterfly, fluttering around without a care in the world. If you asked her how she knew how to climb these cliffs, she would say "When I look at the cliff walls, somehow I just *get* it." It was proof that her incredible powers of observation weren't limited to people.

Soshi was amazed. "Well, that's a shock. I guess I should add 'adventurer' to the list right after 'religious guru.'"

"Seems more up her alley," Kazuki laughed. Soshi gave a curious smile.

"Just as she could have been an adventurer in a perfect world, lots of the kids on this island are gifted. Like Koyo. He and a few other kids always get test papers with different questions than the rest of the class, right?"

"Yeah."

He spoke of a system that was unique to Tatsumiya Island's schools. Their educational policy enforced constant spurring of the more capable students. Depending on the student, they might be placed in a separate class for a given subject, or else given different test questions. There was a brief period when it was popular for students to complain, "Sensei, I got Koyo's test" when test papers were being handed out. In other words, "Sensei, this test is too hard."

Soshi phrased things another way. "Koyo has the mind of a Nobel prize winner. Particularly in mathematics, his mental faculties are abnormally high. Perhaps he could've won a place in history as a famous physician, or maybe an economist or an arms developer."

"Wow..." Kazuki couldn't help but marvel.

Everyone was so gifted.

"You too, Kazuki."

"Me?"

"Your physical prowess is highly developed. Didn't you ever notice?" Soshi said. It seemed like it should have gone without mentioning at this point.

"Eh, well I can run a little faster than the next guy maybe."

"You could win the gold medal in every single Olympic event."

"Oh come on, now! That's going too far."

"I'm serious. As long as you had a rival, you could stretch your abilities to create new world records all over the place."

Kazuki gave him an objectionable look. "Even synchronized swimming?" he asked with a straight face.

"I...I was just being hypothetical," Soshi stammered.

"Huh." It sparked Kazuki's interest just a bit. Synchronized swimming. "So what did you mean by 'special factors'?" It was the burning question. The more he thought about it, the scarier it seemed to be pushing these kids' abilities to the limit like that.

"That's a Level Twenty-One question," Soshi said softly, then fell into silence. It was like trying to explain the customs of one's country to a foreigner. "Your awareness restriction code has only just reached Level Seven. It would probably just cause you unnecessary confusion if I bothered trying to explain it."

Level Seven. Level Twenty-One. Kazuki

reckoned the difference between these two numbers represented the difference in the depth of the darkness they each embraced. If he ever reached that level, he would be able to speak more naturally with Soshi, to say the least.

"Let's get going. The wind is getting chilly. Can you walk?" Soshi stood up. Kazuki quickly did likewise to avoid having Soshi try to lend him a hand. If Soshi had stuck his hand out, Kazuki probably would've frozen with apprehension.

"I'm okay, I can walk." Determined not to lose to the only muscular pain he had ever really felt in his whole life, Kazuki put some strength into his legs and began walking.

They spent the remainder of the journey in silence. It wasn't that they didn't know what to say, but simply that they knew they didn't have to say anything. It was a natural silence.

They walked along the coastline, watching the sun set in opposite part of the sky. The area was still scattered with remains of destruction, the forest of walls had disappeared, and a fraction of the military weapons were still trained on the skies.

Eventually, they arrived at the stone steps leading to Kazuki's home.

"Well, this is my house," Kazuki said, stopping in his tracks.

Soshi knew that much. He gave a little shrug. "Make sure you rest up for a while. I'll come by tomorrow."

"Huh?" Kazuki's eyes widened in surprise.

"Is that weird?"

"Oh, n-no," Kazuki stuttered. Soshi responded with a gentle smile.

"Four years, seven months, and eleven days, huh?"

"Hm?"

"That's what Koyo said, right?"

"Oh, yeah."

It was that morning, when Soshi and Kazuki were trying to leave the classroom together. It was Koyo's own way of pointing out how long it had been since the last time they had done that.

Soshi gave another shrug. "It's just...hard to believe that's all it's been. It felt so much longer," he said softly, gazing out at the sunset sky. His eyes were incredibly distant—both his right eye and his scarred left one.

"Why...?" Kazuki said reflexively. Why hadn't he told anyone Kazuki did it? Why had he kept it a secret until now, and why was he continuing to do so? Why wasn't he saying something this very instant? Kazuki started to ask him, but ultimately hung his head, unable to put it into words.

"Kazuki," Soshi said. Kazuki slowly raised his face to see Soshi, full of emotion, the left side of his face pointed towards him. "Thank you," he said with a smile. It was as if the scar running down his left eye had always been waiting for Kazuki. "Because of you, we were able to protect this island."

"Come on, I didn't do anything..." He was glad and embarrassed at the same time. He could feel his own face turning red. But he knew Soshi was telling him not to worry about things—about the ugliness in his heart that was exposed when he entered the Fafner and destroyed his enemy. In reality, it was only a mentality that had been created by the Nibelung rings. Of course, even if it had been Kazuki's true character, he imagined Soshi would've given him the same smile. That made it all the more embarrassing.

"You're gonna catch a chill," Soshi said as if talking to a little kid. "Hurry up and get inside. And get some rest."

"What about you?"

"I'm going back to Alvis. I'll see you tomorrow."

"Okay."

Soshi turned on his heels and began a hasty return.

Kazuki continued watching him for awhile in a daze, until he remembered he had something to ask.

"Soshi!" he shouted.

Soshi halted in his tracks and spun around. Kazuki took relief in the fact that Soshi had actually responded to his voice. He took in a deep breath, as if preparing for leaping over a five-year gap in a single bound.

"Who'd you bet on?!" he shouted out.

Kazuki's challengers. Who would win and who would lose? Maximum bet two thousand yen.

An amused expression spread across Soshi's face.

"Someday I'll tell you," he shouted back. He too

felt as if he were a distant voice of the past calling out to the present.

Soshi turned once again and gradually disappeared in the distance, choking back laughter as he went. Kazuki kept his eyes on Soshi's back forever.

The next morning, Soshi really did show up at Kazuki's house—and in the morning, no less.

He walked into the entrance. "Good morning, Commander Makabe," he said politely to Kazuki's father in his workshop.

"Just 'Makabe' is fine here," Fumihiko replied.

Kazuki was a bit taken aback. For the time being, he showed Soshi to his room on the second floor and prepared some tea and snacks. "So what's this 'commander' business?" he asked as he brought them in. He furrowed his brow at the thought of his father having some kind of a hidden career.

"He's the battle command post's tactics commander. Hadn't you heard?"

Kazuki shook his head. "Sounds pretty highfalutin."

"Well, in war time he's got top authority, so it *is* highfalutin."

"Even though he's a pot-maker?"

"Nevertheless," Soshi laughed. Kazuki laughed a bit, too.

In reality, having Soshi in his room was a nerve-wracking thing for Kazuki. But as time passed, he began to feel at ease about it.

Mostly they talked about Kuramae. As the adopted daughter of the Minashiro family, she had always been like something of a cousin to Soshi. In both public and private—in both his true life and the one which served this island's façade—she was the one person he could act truly natural with, he said.

Kazuki recalled Kuramae as she turned her back on him in the Bahnzweck. He wanted to say something to that back, to reassure her that Soshi really was grateful for her.

A bit past noon, Soshi headed back to Alvis. Kazuki was informed that there would be no school for the day, and he was still experiencing some gripping pains here and there, so he spent the day loafing in his room.

He knew he probably should have asked his father about some of the circumstances surrounding the island, but he couldn't bring himself to say anything. Something just seemed awkward about the idea of hobbling down the stairs to say, "Hey, Dad, are we at war?"

Instead, he prepared some lunch and called in his father to eat.

"Thanks," Fumihiko said and came into the living room. Usually, he went out for lunch. Occasionally, he felt like he ought to just make it himself, but somehow the look of the bowls always changed his mind. Kazuki also secretly feared the possibility of having to eat the leftovers of his father's cooking.

They ate in silence as usual, until Fumihiko briefly breached it. "How much did you learn about the island?"

"...The sun sets in the east and right now it's September," Kazuki said with similar brevity.

"Huh," he muttered. "If you want to ask something, ask. As long as you don't ask why I never told you, I'll answer anything," he said, and then fell silent again. Kazuki was silent, as well. Fumihiko had just vetoed the very first question on his list.

As he was stacking the dishes after their meal, Kazuki finally thought of a question. "Why...can't I ask why you never told me?"

"I was going to tell you next year. It was our decision to keep silent about it until then." He almost seemed apologetic that Kazuki had ended up discovering the truth about the island. There was something unnerving about having his own father apologize to him.

"Did you know I might end up piloting the Fafner?"

"Yes," Fumihiko said plainly, but something about it sounded like he had just barely managed to squeeze the words out after choking back all of his anger and despair. It was enough for Kazuki to realize that, if he pressed any further, it wouldn't be pretty.

"I'll clean up." Fumihiko picked up the used eating utensils and disappeared into the kitchen. It was a different feeling than when Kuramae had turned her back to Kazuki in the Bahnzweck.

At the same time, the doorbell rang from the entrance. Not knowing who to expect, Kazuki went to greet the visitor.

"It's Kazuki!"

It was Maya. She looked truly glad to see him standing there. It was as if she was afraid he might have turned into a completely different person in the course of a single night.

"Thank God. It's really you. I'm so glad. Oh, I'm sorry. I just came to get a look at you. I've actually got to go help my mom now. So many people were wounded, everything's just crazy now. Sorry. To bother you, I mean. Oh, thank God. Well, see ya. Bye." She went on and on in a single stream, oblivious to how flustered Kazuki had become, and then, in the same breath, left again.

Dumbfounded, Kazuki stayed and watched her as she disappeared into the distance, then made his way to the bathroom.

"This is me, right?" he said, staring deeply into the mirror.

The next morning, there was a funeral ceremony. Due to the extremely high number of deaths, the people of the island all attended a single ceremony together. It was a sight that made it shockingly clear to Kazuki just how many people had perished.

Adorned in funeral attire, he and Soshi made an offering of burning incense in Kuramae's honor.

No tears were shed. And yet their hearts brimmed with feelings of gratitude and apology. Throngs of people stood everywhere, raising cries of grief. The face of Kuramae that the enemy had shown Kazuki came to mind once again, but the fact that it wasn't really her allowed him to keep his emotions suppressed. He wondered how that really could have been himself aboard the Fafner. To him, the idea seemed far beyond his grasp.

There was also the fear that if he really thought about it, it would throw his mind into utter chaos. There were a lot of things he decided he'd better not ponder too deeply.

The next day, he received notice once again that school would be closed. It wasn't that the school had been destroyed or that loads of teachers had died. It was just taking some time to decide on class time slots, they explained.

Time slots? It seemed strange to him. Weren't they already posted on the day of the opening ceremony?

But all of his questions were answered the following day by a single, ordinary letter. It didn't come in the mail bin. His father had come home carrying it just as Kazuki was beginning to wonder where he had gone.

After lunch, his father handed it to him. He opened it to find that the letter itself was tediously written in formal language on pretty red paper. Ignoring most of it, he thumbed through the pages until he came across a time table.

Apparently this was to become his schedule in the event that he answered "Yes" to a certain question. He looked at the first time block. It listed the usual classes like "Foreign Language", "Mathematics", and "Social Studies." Second period and beyond, however, were filled with incomprehensible things like "Alvis Duty Training," "Skill Training," "Equipment Training," and "Primary Subjects."

"What is this?"

"It's a certificate of eligibility to become a pilot. If you agree to the pledge, that's your schedule," Fumihiko said.

Kazuki gave his father a perplexed look. "Why's it red?"

"It's a practice from the old days. Those recruited to be soldiers received a red letter."

"Huh." For no reason in particular, Kazuki flipped the letter over and stared at it for a while on the dining table. "In other words, it's telling me to pilot the Fafner?" he asked.

"It's telling you to *decide* whether you will or not."

This was a surprise. He didn't think he would get a choice. He was expecting to just do whatever Soshi told him—no more, no less.

And yet, at the same time, he didn't think this document really was giving him a choice. He had the faint feeling that he didn't even deserve a right to choose. The document was only a formality, something saying "*You* chose this" so that Kazuki would have to take personal responsibility.

Fumihiko sat and watched Kazuki like this for a while before eventually speaking. "Come with me for a minute."

He rose to his feet and made his way over to the earthen floor of the workshop. Kazuki followed behind. As he wondered what this was about, his father had him take a seat at the pottery wheel, one of the essential tools of the trade. Fumihiko put some clay in front of him and wet his hands.

"Just try it out," he said. "Do whatever you feel like."

As he placed his hands on the rotating clay, Kazuki wondered how he ever managed to keep from becoming a delinquent with a father like this. Doing his best to imitate the way his father always did it, he managed to whip up something to the effect of a bowl. Not half bad, he thought.

"The materialized body of a Festum is ninety-nine percent silicon," Fumihiko suddenly said.

"Huh...? What?" Kazuki couldn't take his eyes off the clay. Now was no time to be telling him cryptic things.

"Silicon. Clay, basically. That's what the enemy's really made of."

As his father spoke these words, Kazuki recalled the crying face of Kuramae, screaming out to him as the black sphere swallowed her up. He recalled the golden enemy, trying to heal him of the very wounds it had inflicted. The extreme feeling of pleasure he felt as he tore the golden shimmering entity to pieces rose once again inside his chest.

"Ah..." He was in a daze. The next thing he knew, the bowl-like object in his hands had turned to a clump of mush. Without even thinking, he had crushed it in his hand. It was as if the clay itself was the enemy.

"The more you fight them, the more warped you'll become." His father's low voice struck his ears so poignantly that it was painful. The pottery wheel stopped spinning. A bit confused, Kazuki looked up at Fumihiko.

"Would you like me to teach you how to touch clay without becoming warped?" Fumihiko said with a gentleness in his voice that Kazuki had never heard before.

There was a fairly long silence before Kazuki responded. That was how long it took him to grasp his father's intention. It was such a roundabout way of saying it that it seemed to prove they were related, Kazuki thought.

In other words, Fumihiko was saying that if Kazuki didn't want to be a pilot, they'd figure something out together.

Kazuki rolled some dried clay around in his hands. "I'm okay for now...but show me someday." He felt somehow embarrassed, and that was all he could manage to say. He wasn't even sure whether he was happy or unhappy, but he wondered why his father was suddenly talking to him when they had practically never had a decent conversation before. "It's just that ...I promised Soshi."

Thinking that made it sound like Soshi was more important than his own father, Kazuki spoke with some reluctance. But, in fact, that might have been the truth.

"I see," Fumihiko said plainly, not sounding particularly disappointed. He went off to wash the dishes, and Kazuki cleaned the bathtub and filled it with hot water. Fumihiko told him to go ahead and take the first bath, so he did. When he was finished, he went out to the hall to say so, but was cut off by the sight of his father standing in the entranceway.

He knew that was where they kept the picture of his mother. Silently, he went upstairs. He couldn't help but be a bit shocked by how terribly small Fumihiko looked as he stared at the image of Kazuki's deceased mother.

The next morning, Kazuki wrote out his "Signature of Consent" and passed it on to his father. Then he left for school for the first time in four days. He climbed up the stone steps and ran into Maya as soon as he reached the sloped path.

"My expectations were a little off. I was going to try and sneak up behind you," Maya laughed. She walked her bike beside him, its tires crackling on the dried asphalt.

"Your place must've been pretty busy, huh?" Kazuki asked.

"They made me help with something every single day. I wanted to come bring you a get-well present, but..."

"I'm not sick."

"Heh, yeah."

Kazuki suddenly remembered the red letter.

"Tomi, are you—" he started, but then cut himself off. But it was enough for her to know what he was going to say.

"I'm not a pilot." She did her best to use what was apparently an unfamiliar word. Perhaps her awareness restriction code hadn't risen that far yet. Or perhaps she simply had no desire to accept that the suddenly transformed world was the real one. Perhaps she wanted to believe that the peaceful days they had lived up to now were the real reality.

But her answer came as a surprise to Kazuki.

"Really?" he said. What about Soshi's explanation? He said they chose pilots based on signs of Savant Syndrome.

"Yeah. I've got a physical handicap, so they said I couldn't board one of those things."

"A handicap?"

"They said I'm perfectly healthy for doing everyday stuff. But I can't be a pilot." Kazuki was in disbelief. This was the girl who climbed up deadly cliff walls like they were ladders. She had a handicap? It sounded like some kind of a joke, but Maya's serious expression made it plenty clear that it was the truth. It seemed like cruel irony that the daughter of a family of doctors should receive such a diagnosis. According to Soshi, the Tomis were charged with the invaluable role of collecting students' physical data for the pilot selection assembly.

"I thought I was totally healthy, so it was a bit of a shock. But I'm pretty relieved, too."

"What handicap? You're not sick, are you?"

"No, it's nothing like that. It's not a matter of getting sick. It's a matter of whether I have what it takes. It's not that my body is weak or anything. It's that my nerves are underdeveloped or something. They say the development of my nerves ended up some way or another and piloting would be inhibited or such and such."

"I...don't get it."

"Yeah, I don't, either. Not even a little bit," Maya snickered. But there was something terribly melancholic about her. The very fact that they were having such a conversation was proof that everything had completely changed. There was nothing they could do, and, like the red letter, they didn't really have any choices.

"Hey, Kazuki-kun? You'll protect them, right?"

"Huh? Who?"

"The people you fight together with. I want you to protect them," Maya said. She was dead serious.

Kazuki recalled Soshi telling him that there were twelve pilots in all. Was she telling him to protect the other eleven by himself? It seemed like an outrageous demand.

"Me?"

"I think you of all people can do it. If you can't, no one can," she said with great certainty. Maya being who she was, and also being a member of the Tomi family, perhaps there were things she knew that Kazuki didn't.

"I'll...do my best," he finally answered. He recalled Soshi's desperation when he tried to get the entrance to Alvis behind the school open. It was such a heavy obligation. Kazuki wondered what it must have felt like to take full responsibility for what happened, with no one else to rely on.

"I'm sorry. But...you're the only one I can ask, Kazuki."

Seeing Maya with her head hung apologetically, Kazuki felt like he had done something wrong.

"I understand. I'll do my best," he said more

firmly. Maya raised her face. She looked like she was on the verge of tears.

"Thank you," she said, trying to force a smile. Kazuki gave his best reliable-looking nod. In reality, he hadn't thought of anything beyond following Soshi's instructions. He was already trying to convince himself that he was fine with what had happened to Kuramae.

Shoko was once again absent from school. Kazuki waved at her as she meekly peered out her window at them, then he headed to school. Nobody else spoke to him the rest of the way. There weren't even any new challenge letters in his shoe cupboard.

Koyo approached him as soon as he walked into class.

"Four days ago was pretty tough, huh?" he said in a low voice.

"Yeah..."

Soshi had recommended that he not let his role as a pilot become public news around school. Koyo did a good job of keeping things vague, as if he knew this.

"You got one too, right? Those papers?"

"What, you mean you did, too?"

"We seem to be very similar as far as those things go."

Kazuki nodded, although it seemed to him that the difference between a letter of challenge and a love letter was pretty great. It was no surprise that Koyo had been chosen as a pilot, though.

"Did you try asking about anything?"

"Huh?"

"It was written on the paper. 'If you have any inquiries, please feel free to ask.' I called just to check it out, and they were pretty nice about telling me whatever I wanted to know."

"Wow."

"Doesn't look like you're interested. Do you know the other pilot candidates?"

"Well, uh..."

It seemed like knowing the other candidates would just make him feel worse. Just remembering Kuramae getting sucked up by that black ball was enough to make the bile rise in his stomach. The thought of having to explain what fate might be in store for the other pilots didn't thrill him.

"I just want to worry about what I'm going to do for now," he said.

"Wow. I wish I were like you." It was a simple offhand comment, but it truly surprised Kazuki.

"Me? Why?"

"I always worry about every tiny little detail, you know? I occasionally disgust myself."

"If it's just 'occasionally,' is it really so bad?"

Koyo gave Kazuki a pat on the shoulder. That was exactly the kind of thing he was talking about.

When first period was over, those students qualified to become pilots left their classrooms and proceeded to Alvis as previously instructed. Students who really became pilots would spend every day like this, only going to school in the morning before heading over to the "special classroom."

Perhaps even the first period class was nothing more than a nicety the adults had provided so the pilots could be with other kids. If so, it was a nicety Kazuki could have lived without.

On that particular day, first period was the only class for all students. The remaining time was spent on what the adults had dubbed "mental care." Students unable to keep up with the sudden extreme changes in their lives could confide in teachers or talk with each other. They could also ask the teachers about the details of the current state of the world. They were essentially free to decide how to use the time. Maya explained all of this to Kazuki later on. As for her, in learning about the current state of the world she was shocked to hear that the Himalayas had been blown away in a battle and were now gone. True to her reputation, Maya said she had wanted to climb them someday.

Leaving the other students behind, Kazuki and Koyo entered Alvis through the entrance behind the school. The debris from the destroyed cistern had neatly disappeared. They used an intercom on the well-maintained entrance to give their names, and then were forced to give their addresses and phone numbers before finally being allowed in.

Once they got down the dark staircase, Kazuki lost his bearings. The path split three ways. All three were open, turning the place into a maze.

"It's this way, Kazuki. You still can't remember the way?" Koyo was referring to the hypnotic memorization they had undergone. For Kazuki, any information scrolling through his head without a recognizable image attached just seemed like a meaningless string of symbols. It seemed that as long as Koyo had these symbols, he was set. He led the way to the elevator without getting lost, and they descended underground. Apparently, he was much more adjusted to the situation than Kazuki. He could use the word "Alvis" in a conversation without a hint of awkwardness, and in explaining what they would be doing from now he had used several other strange words.

Getting out of the elevator, they found themselves in the lobby. In the hallway, there were a row of entrances that appeared to lead to small meeting rooms. They were each invited into one of the rooms by the adults.

Kazuki figured this was where everyone who would become a pilot was gathered, but he was completely wrong. Throughout the day, adult after adult came to talk to Kazuki alone. They said it was to clarify differences between the pilot candidates and that it wouldn't take long, but they didn't let him leave until nine hours later.

First, they made him confirm whether or not he wanted to become a pilot a countless number of times, using every possible phrasing. Then, they explained in detail what restrictions, special privileges, and duties he would have if he became a pilot. He felt like they were telling him over and over not to become one. And then came the tests, which to him made no sense whatsoever.

For example:

Asked to draw a tree on a piece of paper, Kazuki drew a blazing red one, to which the test proctor responded with a fascinated expression.

For example:

Asked to put a set of randomly arranged numbers in numerical order within twenty seconds, Kazuki managed to do it in just under five, to which the test proctor again responded with a fascinated expression.

For example:

Asked to say the first word that came to mind after seeing a picture of an elderly man who had been hit by a truck, Kazuki answered with "Mach Five," to which the test proctor responded with a deep nod. Kazuki wanted to ask why he was nodding but stayed silent.

And so nine hours passed. They provided lunch midway through, during which the adults came to Kazuki with many things to say. The one thing that bothered him was that there was an enormous mirror on one of the walls. He couldn't help but imagine there were loads of people on the other side watching his every move as he ate lunch and conversed.

That might have really been the case, but Kazuki decided not to think about it. Meanwhile, the adults asked him this and that about his personal life, and it wasn't long before the topic of his dreams came up. The person in charge skillfully led the conversation so that Kazuki would go into more detail about his dream of swimming in the dark ocean.

"You don't ever think to return to the light?"

"Probably not. It's impossible, after all."

"It's not that somebody is forbidding it, but

rather that you yourself think it's impossible, right?"

"Yes. Um, is that weird?"

"Certainly not. That dream is one of the reasons you're able to pilot a Fafner."

"It is?"

"Your dream is what's called a 'borderline.'"

Kazuki was at a loss for words. He never would've guessed his dream had a name. But then again, even that jet-black machine he had gotten in had a name. Maybe it wasn't so strange for a dream to have one, too.

"When your sense of self is uncertain, you are in an energy-producing state, but also in an energy-losing state. It is because your mind is still developing that you are able to synchronize so smoothly with the Fafner."

Kazuki just shook his head in silence. He wasn't following along very well. If Soshi had told him the same thing, he might have nodded in silence instead. But the one in charge here wasn't Soshi, and nobody asked why Kazuki had come to have dreams like this.

At the end of the day, they explained what would be going on from now on.

"When two people fight as a single unit, it's called a 'Twin Dog.' This is a fundamental Fafner battle formation. A single pilot in battle is called a 'Lone Dog.' The unit is completely without backup support, and must support the entire burden with his or her own abilities alone. As a result, this formation is rarely implemented."

Kazuki, whose first battle had been in the Lone Dog formation, simply nodded in silence.

"When three people fight as a single unit, it's called a 'Triple Dog,' and four people is a 'Cross Dog.' This is a fundamental of cooperative action. All twelve Fafner units battling together is reffered to as an 'Alto Dog,' and that is the formation you will all be aiming for in training. In the beginning phase, you will each be assigned partners."

"Partners?"

"In order to create Twin Dog formations. You will all undergo training to learn how to work in pairs, to stay aware of one another, and to support one another in order to create an advantage on the battleground."

"You mean to synchronize with our partners?"

"Likewise, they will synchronize with you. It's a mutual setup."

Cooperate with someone else? Kazuki felt like she had just assigned him the most difficult task in the world.

"Um...so we're not allowed to fight alone?"

The one in charge grinned and shook her head. "Out of the question."

This was just about as shocking to him as when the enemy invaded.

Why does it have to be this way? he wondered, as the weight of the world seemed to crush him from above.

"Out of the total twenty-three pilot candidates, we have one official decision, eleven primary candidates, eight secondary candidates, three tertiary candidates, and the remaining ten are backup candidates," Koyo said inside the Bahnzweck. Both he and Kazuki were determined not to show any surprise or discomfort at the fact that they were traveling underwater. They were trying to act as if it wer something to be taken for granted. That was how everyone was attempting to accept the current circumstances. They swallowed their sense of discomfort and told themselves that all of this was natural.

Aside from Kazuki and Koyo, several other students were aboard the Bahnzweck, having left school after first period to assemble for training. They were currently on their way to the training ground.

"You're the only one they've decided on so far, Kazuki," Koyo whispered praisingly.

"Huh."

"Come on, show a little pride. Those 'backup candidates' they mentioned are the people who didn't even get one of those red papers."

"Huh? They didn't?"

"They're applicants," Koyo said with a fairly serious expression.

"Applicants?"

Kazuki wanted to ask why, but couldn't get the words out. He knew that many of the people who died in the first attack must have had children or siblings who wanted to funnel their anger and hate into some kind of action.

"Almost time for skill training. I could get switched to a secondary candidate depending on my marks."

Kazuki didn't know anything and didn't particularly care, but he gave his opinion to be polite. "Come on, you're not going to be switched." It was his true opinion. Koyo shrugged, as if he kind of agreed.

"It's just that I hear they do make people switch units in some cases."

"Switch units?"

"You're the pilot of Mark Elf, right?"

"Yeah."

"That's a power model that excels in close combat on the ground. My Mark Vier is a speed model designed for diversion tactics and scouting."

"Huh. So they're each different."

"Yeah, exactly. That's also how they determine who your partner will be. The Twin Dog formation is based on the combined abilities of the units rather than the differences between pilots."

"Wow. So the pairs are actually predetermined?"

"Pretty much. And, depending on grades, I could end up riding in your unit." Buried within Koyo's smile was an expression Kazuki had never seen before. It was the face his challengers always made shortly before a match.

"You want to ride in the Mark Elf?"

Koyo shrugged and smiled, but didn't answer. Kazuki asked a different question.

"What color is Mark Vier?"

"Blue-gray. It's a little dark, and more on the blue side. I guess you could call it 'deep' blue."

"I'm not a fan of blue, so you're out of luck,"

Kazuki said with a straight face. Koyo frowned. But in all seriousness, Kazuki somehow felt like the pitch black unit belonged to him. That was undoubtedly an essential factor in unifying with the Fafner. Most important of all, however, was the fact that it was Soshi who had asked him to board the machine in the first place. He didn't want to give it up, even for Koyo.

"Koyo, do you really want to pilot a Fafner?" he asked again. It was nearly impossible to imagine Koyo exchanging blows with an enemy.

"My parents...they were so happy." Koyo narrowed his eyes and gave a light smile. There was something very reserved about it. Surely it would've been irresistible to the girls, but to Kazuki it was disturbing enough to wipe the smile clean off his own face. Koyo knew all too well just how little his parents cared about him. He also knew how much he wanted them to.

"When they saw the red letter that day, they said...it had been worth raising me all these years."

Kazuki furrowed his brow. Koyo stared out the window of the Bahnzweck as it continued through the sea.

"They say Japan is gone."

"Yeah." Kazuki looked out at the ocean as well. The dark ocean, the same color as the darkness that so many people had embraced. "And here we thought we were both getting out of here in a year. Sure didn't see this coming." It was a laughable thought that no one could possibly laugh at, but Kazuki did his best to make it sound lighthearted.

"Was it scary getting in the Fafner?"

"Yeah. But it wasn't so scary once I was inside. Sure hurt, though."

"Haha. None of that suits me too well."

"Yeah, not really my cup of tea, either."

"I know." Koyo said with a gentle smile. The next thing he said came out as a whisper. "It must be scary to fight the enemy, huh?"

"Soshi probably knows how to beat them. I just have to do as he says." Those were Kazuki's true feelings on the matter. He didn't know anything else about it. It didn't matter if he didn't win. If Soshi gave an order, he would follow it. Anything else was beyond his control. That was what he really believed. It was the only thing he could rely on in this newly transformed world.

"I envy you," Koyo said with a grin. "You know I really always wanted to be like you."

"Why?" Kazuki asked with a troubled expression. Koyo snickered at him.

"I take it you haven't looked at the pairs chart yet, either? For the Twin Dogs, I mean."

Kazuki obviously hadn't even known it existed.

"Please protect her," Koyo suddenly said.

"Huh?" Hadn't he heard something like that before?

"I might be useless, but I know you can keep her safe."

At some point, Koyo's smile had disappeared, replaced with a terribly serious, somehow melancholy expression. It was the face of someone who realized his own helplessness.

"Please..."

Why? Who? Kazuki wanted to ask, but he was stunned by Koyo's sudden change of demeanor. Suddenly, he thought of Maya. Right. She had said the same thing to him. To protect the people he fought together with.

Did everyone think he was so suited for combat? As he felt a flashback to himself tearing apart the enemy coming on, he gritted his teeth. He could feel the presence of a frightfully violent impulse deep within his heart. He knew it was there.

Nobody wanted to become like that. Maybe if someone had to do it, he was the one for it. Somehow that made sense to him.

" ...Sure thing," he said.

I'll take in all of the fear and pain so that you don't have to fight. Because I'm fine. I can give scars and take them.

Koyo gave a silent nod and continued staring into the darkness of the ocean.

They got off the Bahnzweck and parted ways, each heading to their respective designated place. Kazuki took an elevator to the lower block and a supervisor directed him to a place that appeared to be a medical room. In the room, they took his pulse and did a simple physical checkup, then made him remove his clothes. When he was fully naked, they made him walk down a hallway lit by blue-white light. The light was coming from a sterilization lamp. At the same time, he was blasted with warm air to rid his body of bacteria and dust. He got the feeling he had seen something like this in a movie, where a prisoner had to walk down a hall getting sprayed with a hose instead of getting to take a shower. But wait—that was prison.

It also occurred to him that this was probably the first time he had ever been forced to walk ten meters in the nude in his whole life. He involuntarily picked up the pace of his step, and by the last meter he had become fairly desperate to get his clothes back on. Perhaps that was what they were going for.

That would certainly explain the outrageous clothing awaiting him at the end of this nude footrace. It was known as the "Synergetic Suit." It was skin-tight, and it exposed parts of the arms, belly, and thighs. Those were exactly the places where the seat inside the cockpit connected to the pilot.

The word *synergetic* referred to the suit's role in linking and stimulating a specific type of nerve cells in the brain known as insulated neurons. It was the key to uniting Fafner and pilot. Once connected, the pilot's entire nervous system was bound with the Fafner's.

The psychological state of a pilot linked with a Fafner was known was the "Synergetic Code." In order to reach this state, it was necessary for all brain waves in all parts of the brain—from the outer layer "topsoil" responsible for producing our "humanness" to the more primitive "Dark Floor" deep within, which housed the R-complex—to be strictly in tune. When those brainwaves had attained a connection at the "Golden Ratio," it was displayed on a brain scanner to indicate that the pilot had entered a state of connectivity, known as an algorithmic spiral. Without achieving this state, the Fafner was just a robot. In other words, it would be about as easy to operate as a clunky crane. If a Synergetic Code was formed, however, the need to operate it disappeared completely. This was because the pilot *became* the Fafner. They simply had to do what they had been learning to do non-stop since they were babies—that is, walking, jumping, holding objects, and so forth.

All of this information flickered through Kazuki's mind as he tugged his suit on. In reality, though, it was all irrelevant to him. He was able to open the Fafner's eyes from the moment he had entered the cockpit on Soshi's orders. In Kazuki's mind, it was no big deal, just like beating the second place runner in a marathon by over a minute was no big deal. He wasn't conscious of the fact that he had formed a Synergetic Code or that this was the product of his natural talents.

And so Kazuki donned his suit, convincing himself that it was no different from wearing a bathing suit to take the edge off the embarrassment. Exiting the changing room, he thought impersonally about how hard it must have been for the girls. Considering the electric chair shock that came with entering the pilot seat and the feeling of suspension in mid-air that followed it, it seemed only natural that all the pilots would be boys. Boys were the only ones present on the Bahnzweck as well. What Kazuki didn't know, however, was that boys and girls were only separated until they had donned their suits. He would discover this at the commencement of training.

The supervisor was a woman, and she made no comments about how the suit looked on him. She simply gave dry instructions. Perhaps she was thinking about it on the inside, but she kept quiet about it.

She brought Kazuki to a place known as the Simulation Room. It was about the size of a classroom, and had an enormous screen taking up an entire wall. There were two silver-colored eggs on the floor. They were simulation cockpit blocks that used an electronic program to mimic the sensation of being in a real Fafner.

The supervisor instructed Kazuki to wait beside the simulation cockpits and left the room for a moment. Soon after, as Kazuki was staring at his own goofy reflection in the egg-like cockpit, she returned with another pilot candidate in tow.

Slender as a stem and just as delicate, the candidate's perfectly fitted suit nonetheless exposed an unbelievably soft-looking array of curves. Kazuki took one look at her and then did a double take.

"Well then, please introduce yourself to your partner," the supervisor said. She didn't say who should start, but her face was pointed towards the one who had arrived late, and she gave a little indicative nod. She gave off an air of encouragement, as if to remind the cowering candidate that first impressions were the most important.

"Um, I'm pl-pleased to be w-working with you." The girl had desperation written all over her bright red face as she bowed to him. When she looked up at Kazuki again, her face turned even redder. It took all of

her effort to squeeze out her glass musical instrument of a voice. "I...I'm Shoko Hazama, p-pilot candidate for M-Mark Sechs," she said in a single breath. She looked at him with insecure eyes, as if she had delivered the line better when she practiced it at home.

The supervisor nodded at Kazuki as if to say, "Look at this girl. At least give her a smile, will you?" But of course he was unable to deliver a smile or any other clever form of response, and just barely managed to give an awkward bow instead.

Wondering if there hadn't been some sort of mistake, he looked up again to see that Shoko Hazama really was standing there.

"Kazuki Makabe, pilot of the Mark Elf," he said in a voice that was for some reason even softer than his partner's.

Most of the first day of training was spent on meditation. This was so the candidates could get a feel for the moment of unification with the Fafner inside the cockpit.

"Clench your teeth. This will hurt a bit," the supervisor's voice resonated throughout the cockpit just as the lid was shut. Kazuki slid his fingers through the rings of the simulation Nibelung System and clenched his molars to brace for the shock. Linking devices snapped around his chest, belly, and legs as an electric jolt ran through his whole body. The phrase "electric chair" did not come to mind. It was a considerably weaker shock than the first time. He knew why right away. The suit had taken the edge off, and the formation of a Synergetic Code had made it easy for Kazuki's nervous system to unify with that of the Fafner's.

Shoko, however, was a concern. Kazuki wondered if the shock might have made her pass out. It seemed that the supervisor was wondering the same thing.

"Are you okay, Hazama-san? Can you respond?" Kazuki could hear the supervisor's voice in his own cockpit as well. There was a brief silence, and then a curious voice cut in.

"Am I...huh? Yes, I'm fine." Apparently she didn't think much of the pain after all. The supervisor was discernibly relieved, and Kazuki was a bit surprised. Shoko was pretty tough, he thought. In time he would learn that she was actually the bearer of a near-inhuman threshold for pain. The moment she realized something hurt, she could just toss her consciousness somewhere else and completely ignore the pain.

This became clear during meditation. The purpose of meditation was to place pilots in the optimum state of readiness for unification with the Fafner. It loosened the muscles in their arms and legs and eased the mental burden by softening neural activity, thereby acting as the first step towards unification. Their muscles would feel warm and flexible, and blood flow would improve. They would feel great comfort and relaxation in the very act of breathing as they fell deeper and deeper into a meditative state. They would feel their hearts beating with perfect rhythm, and entrust their entire bodies to that rhythm, thereby sharpening their involuntary nervous system, stimulating, for example, the nerves in the digestive tract, which normally only work during sleep. The body would start to feel hot as the brain itself shut off.

"Okay. Open your eyes."

As instructed, Kazuki unified his eyesight with that of the Fafner.

And he could see. Standing in front of him was the pure white Mark Sechs unit. The perfect counterpart for the jet-black Mark Elf, it was slender and delicate as a swan. Surprisingly, it also had wings. Kazuki realized this was probably the real reason it reminded him of a swan.

Of course, neither unit was really there. They were the products of an electronic program created for image training. But they sure looked like the real things.

"Now then, please tell your partner your impressions of them."

Kazuki was instructed to go first. He spoke honestly about what he thought of his partner. He said that she was like a white bird and pretty and fragile-looking. The supervisor instructed him to address his partner as "You, the Mark Sechs" with each comment. This was to encourage mutual awareness of her unification with the unit by affirming that she in fact *was* the Mark Sechs.

Shoko—the Mark Sechs—in turn described Kazuki's Mark Elf as black and lizardy and pointy and scary, but added that he looked strong and reliable and was like her exact opposite.

After that, the supervisor had them stand in a

line together and try walking. Kazuki *was* Mark Elf and Shoko *was* Mark Sechs. It was something natural, to be taken for granted.

They were further encouraged to deepen their mutual awareness of each other through physical actions such as shaking hands and patting each other on the shoulder. It was a form of two-way communication that allowed the two partners to support one another. If the two fell out of this mutually aware status at any time, it was known as an "energy loss," and whichever pilot was responsible for it would be removed as a threat to the whole mission, regardless of how skilled he or she might be.

The supervisor was notably surprised— delighted, even—by their speedy ability to complete the first phase of unification with their Fafners. From there, they commenced image development training.

"Jump as high as you think you can," she instructed. Even after unifying with the Fafner, any thoughts like "I can't jump this high" could create a mental contradiction. In reality, even a small hop in the Fafner would send it five meters high. If the pilots let the change in scenery in that moment—the sight of trees and buildings getting smaller and smaller—shake their sense of reality, their unity with the Fafner would dissolve. If they weren't totally convinced that they could jump tens of meters in the air, they wouldn't be able to harness the abilities of the unit.

Kazuki managed to leap more than one hundred twenty meters high. Of course this was only an image. It didn't mean that the Mark Elf could really jump that high, but rather that this was the highest Kazuki could jump without breaking his sense of reality. As a result, a twenty-meter bound in the real Fafner would pose no threat to his sense of unity.

"Amazing. Mark Sechs, go next if you please."

Kazuki stared hard at the white unit as it bowed at the knees. Observing each other's movements was essential in encouraging a mutual unification with their machines.

"H-here I go," Shoko—the Mark Sechs—said.

A moment later, the white unit had completely disappeared from Kazuki's view. By the time he jerked his head upward to look, she was nothing but a dot in the sky.

She really is a bird, Kazuki thought in amazement.

Shoko didn't jump—she flew.

On her very first day, Shoko had nailed an altitude record of seven thousand meters.

"Is she gonna come down?" Kazuki asked the supervisor as Shoko continued to soar.

After several dozen seconds, the Mark Sechs finally fluttered gracefully to the ground. Kazuki could feel the wind as she folded her wings up. She wasn't a bird—she was an angel. It was such a graceful landing, how could Kazuki think anything else?

"You're not a pilot candidate. You're our pilot." The supervisor was overjoyed.

"Incredible," Kazuki said. Shoko was "incredibly" glad.

"I...I think I can go higher," Shoko said, as if she

thought that was what Kazuki wanted.

And, in fact, maybe she could. Kazuki's sensations were all centered on physical movement such as running along the ground, swimming in the ocean and so forth. Shoko, on the other hand, experienced something completely different, in a wholly separate dimension from things like weight and physical strength.

Shoko's fundamental strength lay in her ability to sink into her own imagination. She could readily imagine she was flying through the sky. It wasn't "I can fly." It was "I am flying." The difference between the two was quite literally the difference between Heaven and Earth. Thinking you *can* fly is to recall that you *did* fly. It's an acknowledgment of the fact that you have flown. But if you can accept that you *are* flying, you're already in that state before you take off. Then, it's just a matter of letting reality catch up.

It was Shoko's actions during Pain Training that revealed the true fearsomeness of her power of imagination. Pain Training was essential in stimulating unification with the Fafner as well as improving one's physical abilities. Here Kazuki learned that, in reality, pain performs a vital task in operating the human body. It is largely in charge of judging how our bodies move and what state they are in.

Thus, the Fafner and pain had an inseparable relationship with one another, and in order to pilot a Fafner, one had to accept pain. This was what separated the Fafner from other machines. If your unit were destroyed, your mind would process it as pain.

As a result, it was necessary for pilots to repeatedly undergo unpleasant training to see how much pain they could endure. If they didn't know their own pain thresholds and strive to raise them, even a small amount of damage would be detrimental to the pilot's sense of unity with the Fafner.

But they wouldn't be going through torture or anything. Positioned in front of a single thick wall, they were instructed to push on it. If they thought it hurt, they were free to stop. They pushed with various parts of their bodies, including their arms, elbows, knees, and head.

Kazuki didn't stop pushing even after both his elbows felt like they had dislocated.

"Okay, that's enough. Stop," the supervisor said.

Next, Shoko—the Mark Sechs—placed both her hands on the wall in a similar fashion, and pushed.

"Oof..." she groaned. Both arms cracked as soon as she started pushing. Her head knocked straight into the wall with a clang and partially caved in.

"Stop at once!!" the supervisor yelled.

The Mark Sechs' vision went staticky for a moment, and then cleared up as the unit's frame restored itself. The supervisor had reset the program, returning her to normal.

"Are you still with us? Can you respond?!" the supervisor shouted. Kazuki stared at Mark Sechs, aghast.

"Huh? I...uh, yes. I'm here."

It seemed she didn't understand why the supervisor was scolding her. Had she done something wrong? She didn't even seem to notice she had broken both her arms and bashed her head in.

"You're...experiencing   pain   right   now, correct?"

"Um, yes. But...we're supposed to endure it...right?" Shoko replied feebly. The supervisor was at a loss for words.

Kazuki could hardly believe it, either. Later on, he would learn that this was the result of the same ability that allowed her to soar through the air. By preoccupying herself with the notion that she was "in pain," she could pass through the moment as something that she had already experienced. Then it was just a matter of whether or not reality could catch up—whether it could deliver pain so intense it was deadly. And if that time did come, pain would already have completely vanished from her consciousness. Then it would just be a matter of dying.

If she hadn't actually felt such pain before, she wouldn't have possessed this incredible endurance. Kazuki wondered in complete awe just what kind of intense pain this girl had gone through in her life. At the same time, he felt an incredibly deep darkness.

"You can, without a doubt, operate the Mark Sechs...," the supervisor said. She sounded like she was in the middle of a nightmare.

"Thanks very much!" Kazuki and Shoko thanked each other properly at the end of the first day of training.

"Thank you very much!" they then said while

bowing to the somewhat stunned supervisor. They went to their respective changing rooms and changed back into their own clothes.

"Um..." Shoko stopped Kazuki as he was about to leave. "Could we..."

"Sure," Kazuki answered immediately. There were only three Bahnzweck cars, and once they all left for the other side of the island, all you could do was wait for them to come back. It was just like a train. If Kazuki went ahead and jumped on, there would be one less car. If the other two were gone as well, Shoko would be stuck waiting on the platform.

"Let's go," he said, realizing the need to hurry.

"Um..." Shoko shot him a concerned look, wondering if he really understood what she was trying to say.

"We're going home...together...right?" Kazuki said, shooting back an equally concerned look.

It would've been fairly embarrassing if he had misunderstood her.

"Yeah. Yeah, yeah, yeah," Shoko said, nodding profusely.

Kazuki was a bit relieved. Then he thought of something else.

"Uh, can you walk?" he asked.

"Huh?" she said with a woeful expression. Was *that* how he saw her?

"I mean, I can carry you again..." Kazuki said, trying to be kind.

"I...don't like being carried."

For Shoko, it was an unusually firm assertion.

That was how much she disliked it.

"Sorry." He suddenly felt like he had wronged her. "Bring you, I mean," he rephrased.

"Uhh..." Shoko sounded like a cat stuck between a rock and a hard place. He could tell she was still far from satisfied.

"I mean *hold* you," he tried again, fairly confident that this was the girliest word he could've used.

"Huh...?" This time, it looked like she might go for it. But she snapped back to her senses and shook her head. "I...I can walk by myself."

I'll cry, she seemed to be communicating nonverbally.

"Don't push yourself," Kazuki said.

"I'm not. Not at all."

"Well, okay then." Overruled, Kazuki turned on his heels.

"Um, don't go too fast."

"How's this?"

"A little slower."

"Okay, how's this?"

"Yeah, that's good," Shoko said with a happy grin.

Kazuki scratched his head and fought the urge to mention that it would've been faster to just carry her.

Kazuki had wondered if someone would be waiting on the platform, but ultimately no one was. There were two Bahnzweck cars, so they boarded the closer one. The instant they approached the doors,

You're like a kid.

Kuramae's voice popped to mind. Her laugh as Kazuki peered out at the ocean with his knees on the seat. Her streaming tears as she pushed forth every ounce of courage so as not to lose to the fear and despair of being devoured by the black orb.

"Kazuki-kun?" Shoko asked with concern, jarring him back to his senses. He had frozen in front of the open doors.

"It's nothing." They entered the car, and Kazuki scanned the seats. He wondered where the safest place was. Where could they sit that would allow them to survive? Every seat looked equally safe and equally dangerous. Kazuki forced himself to stop thinking and took a seat in the center of the car. The more you thought about things, the scarier they seemed. It was best to just throw thinking out the window. That also meant acceptance. It meant swallowing down the circumstances and accepting them as nature.

"Uh, um..." Shoko said, still standing up. "May I...sit next to you?"

The doors sealed shut with a smooth sound. Kazuki responded with his own question. "Why are you being so polite?"

"I...I'm sorry."

"It's okay." He tried to show that he wasn't angry. "Isn't it dangerous to be standing up?" he asked.

"Huh?"

Whoosh. The vehicle took off.

"Ah!!"

As expected, the force of the acceleration caused her delicate stem of a body to buckle backwards. With lightning-fast judgment, Kazuki jumped to his feet and grabbed her arm. But then, fearing that tugging on an arm this slender might dislocate it, he took another step forward and placed his other hand on her back. Dipping forward, he managed to prevent her from crashing to the floor. As he mustered every ounce of strength in his body to keep from falling along with her, Kazuki felt like he had seen this pose somewhere before. It wasn't long before he thought of what it was. Ah, that was it. A finishing pose they use in ballet when two people are dancing together. The woman is nearly parallel to the floor while the man has his face intensely close to hers as he supports her.

It was exactly that pose.

As this was running through Kazuki's mind, Shoko was in her own incredible state. Her face was a never-before-trodden shade of red that pushed the boundaries of human face-redness, and her eyes were wide open, perfect circles, like the eyes of a kitten being sniffed by a Doberman. Unable to bat a single eyelash, she just stared at Kazuki's face, which was so close that the slightest nudge would have had them bumping noses. Her lips quivered as she wondered whether they should be open or closed at a time like this.

"Yeah, you'd better take a seat, or else you'll fall," Kazuki said as the force of acceleration began to fade. He finally rose back up. His abnormal leg and back strength were certainly praiseworthy.

"Aahhh..." Shoko replied with all the spirit of an

overboiled stick of asparagus. For the time being, he sat her down on the seat and sat himself down next to her.

"Tired from training?" he asked, glancing up at her slouching body.

Drained, she didn't even seem to understand his question, but nodded anyway.

"Get some sleep."

The Bahnzweck wasn't moving as fast as it had during wartime. It would be another fifteen minutes before they reached the main island. Even a few minutes' sleep should be enough to revitalize her a little bit, he thought.

"Okay..."

Shoko did as she was told. It was true that she was exhausted from training. She had undergone a great deal of overlapping trauma, and at this point she was ready to just pass out. Kazuki felt like a weight had been taken off his shoulders as she conked out like a light. He sighed unintentionally as he looked out the window at the ocean.

Please protect her.

He recalled what Maya and Koyo had both told him. He must have been the only one who didn't know. That she was a pilot candidate. That they would be training partners. That they would be fighting side-by-side if she was said to possess the credentials to participate in real combat.

He didn't know whom he'd end up fighting with. He didn't want to know. He just wanted to follow Soshi's orders. To him, it made far more sense to fight the war alone. He knew that the most difficult thing in the world was being demanded of him—to adapt to another person and have that person adapt to him. And there was no running away. On the contrary, it was swimming away from the light that had brought him here. That inconceivable light.

Shoko?

The thought popped into his head completely without warning.

What in the world? he asked himself.

Kasugai-kun likes someone else.

They were Maya's words. The girl Koyo liked—it was Shoko?

To Kazuki, it seemed like an incoherent string of thoughts. He wasn't used to making deductions based on circumstantial evidence. But now, he felt like he had grasped a flawless answer.

He recalled Koyo's gaze when he called himself useless.

So that was why he was talking about the possibility of piloting the Mark Elf. But Koyo had asked Kazuki to take care of her. He had left in Kazuki's hands something so precious that he would never recover if something were to happen to it.

"Koyo..." he whispered unconsciously.

Idiot. We just happened to be paired together. What do you want me to do? I can't protect her with feelings like yours.

Maya's face came to mind. His sense of calm when she was around. He wasn't sure why, and he didn't care to think about it too deeply. He just sunk himself into his seat and considered confiding in Soshi about everything. He wanted to ask him to let him fight alone. But a number of adults had already told him that was impossible.

Still, somehow he wanted to be alone.

Just then, something hit his shoulder.

It was Shoko's head, leaning on him. By this single action, he had lost the ability to move. If he moved even a little bit, he would probably wake her, and he reckoned the right thing to do was to let her sleep. He took the situation extremely seriously. Pushing the flexibility of his neck muscles to the limit, he turned his head and looked at her face to make sure that she was still breathing.

She was a strangely adorable creature. So this was Koyo's kind of girl, Kazuki thought. She slept like a peaceful, gentle little animal.

An instant later—

"Meat," she said.

For a moment Kazuki actually wondered who might have been speaking.

"Huh??"

"Bwah?" Shoko opened her sleepy eyes.

There was a slurping noise. Kazuki did his best not to imagine what it was.

Shoko confirmed her surroundings in a daze, eventually grasping that she was aboard the Bahnzweck with Kazuki next to her, and that she had been asleep.

"Eeyah!" she shrieked as she clamored to her feet and turned her back to Kazuki, frantically wiping her face—and clearly it was an altogether different part than the one Kuramae had wiped in this very vehicle. It was her mouth.

"...Meat?" Kazuki repeated what he had heard. Shoko's head snapped back around. It was a panicked expression of protest, and the most uppity he had ever seen on her.

"I didn't...say that. I didn't."

"Uhh..."

"Huh?"

"You'd better stay seated. I think."

She inched her way back over and sat down next to him.

"Are you hungry?"

"Mm."

"Do you want to eat meat?"

"I can't," she said with a pained expression and nearly inaudible voice. "But I do like it. I'm sorry," she said with a head bow.

"...My fault."

Kazuki felt ridiculously thickheaded and clumsy. Of course, he probably was. Surely Koyo would've been able to smoothly calm her down.

"No," Shoko said, shaking her head.

They both sat in silence. Neither of them could think of the right thing to say. Eventually, the Bahnzweck reached the main island.

"I...have a bad liver," Shoko said as they were about to get off. She almost sounded embarrassed about it, like it would make people dislike her.

Kazuki did the only thing he could do: show her that he didn't hate her. In fact, he was interested.

"You do?"

Matching his pace to hers while she matched

hers to his, she told him all about her illness as they walked home.

She told him that she was born with a deformed liver that didn't work properly. That sometimes it hurt so badly that she wanted to die. That she couldn't eat things that put stress on her liver very often. Meat, in particular, was mostly off-limits. But, when she was a kid, she was allowed to eat hamburger meat on her birthday, and to her it was unfathomably delicious.

She told him that there were times when she wasn't allowed to eat, no matter how starved with hunger she was. During those times, all she could think about was the hamburger she had eaten as a child and the *yakiniku* she had eaten when she was a little older, and that it was the worst feeling in the world. That she felt pathetic for thinking about meat all day long even though she was a girl.

She also talked about how she relied on her imagination to get through the hard times. For example, she would imagine she was one of the birds she saw flying past her window and think, "I'm flying." Or she would imagine she had eaten so much she was too full to move. Or that she had just finished exercising like crazy with sweat dripping off her and she was walking home from school with a friend.

Or she might even imagine she was already dead. Gone. She had turned to ash and was cast out to sea, or lay in the forest, being eaten by birds.

And so she who had been born wrong would return

to the earth. She prayed that next time she would come out right. When she imagined herself scattering into a million particles of dust, she felt an incredible sense of relief.

Kazuki occasionally piped in with brief responses as he listened. He walked slowly (possibly for the first time in his life) next to her as they made their way through the tunnels of Alvis and climbed the staircase one step at a time. Kazuki noticed the details of his surroundings for the first time, and realized how fast he usually traveled through the place.

"But other than my liver, I'm healthy," Shoko said. "That's the only thing. It's just misshaped. Everything else is fine. So I'm sure I can pilot that thing...the Fafner." It sounded like she was trying to convince herself, as well. "It's the first time anybody's ever told me...I'm the only one who can do it."

"Mm-hm."

"I'm sure I can fly it. For sure."

"Mm-hm," Kazuki replied, trying as hard as he could to do so in a way that would put her mind at ease. A smile spread across Shoko's face, suggesting he had succeeded.

"After we carry out this operation, I wonder if it'll all be over," Shoko said softly as she strolled along the sloped path beneath a sunset sky. "After training, after the battle, once the island moves to someplace safe..."

That was the essential outline of what the adults kept referring to as "this operation." They were going to relocate the island, which had already been discovered by the enemy. They were expecting an enemy assault in the meantime. They would engage the enemy, and as long as they managed to get the island to a safe place, they would be able to return to their peaceful lives.

The phrase of the day for the adults had been "cover every base." The same motto had been Kazuki's key to victory in Ocean Baseball, in a manner of speaking. But apparently the adults' definition of the expression involved placing sick young girls through battle training.

In all honesty, it seemed amazing to Kazuki. On the very first day of training, with no idea what tomorrow might bring, Shoko was thinking about the future. Kazuki, on the other hand, wasn't even trying to think about what lay ahead. The very notion that sooner or later he would be in battle again was suffocating, so he had simply thrown thinking out the window altogether.

"You're amazing, Shoko. Seriously, I think you're incredible," he said. Somehow saying her name just felt natural.

Having suddenly received a compliment, Shoko's face turned bright red, all the way up to her ears. "Oh, I...I guess people don't usually think about stuff like that on the first day, but...I just thought...once the operation is over, maybe we won't get to walk together like this." Her speech was jerky, like someone trying and failing to come to a stop as their feet rushed them down a steep hill. "Because, well, I've always...liked...you, so..." She seemed to realize that the cat was out of the bag, and her voice lost momentum.

"Why?" he asked, surprised.

He was even more taken aback than when Koyo

revealed he wanted to be like him.

"I mean…You can run so fast. And you gave me a lift that time, and..."

"You mean when I carried you?"

"N-no." This conversation again? "Two years ago...when we first entered junior high school."

Hm? He searched through his memory. Had there been a time like that?

"I...wanted to go to school so bad, to see everyone, and..."

Aha, he thought. It was the opening assembly for junior high. He had forgotten something and rushed back to his house. He seemed to recall that it was his indoor shoes or nametag or something that would've made him stand out like an idiot. He imagined the uncomfortable situation he would find himself in if it caught everybody's attention and Soshi saw him. So he ran back home, and on his hurried return back to school again he spotted Shoko crouched on the side of the road, looking deathly ill. The doctor at Tomi Hospital had forbidden her from attending school that day, her mother had told her to stay home and rest, and even Maya had reminded her that she couldn't go to school, but she wanted to go no matter what. She was fine as far as leaving the house, but her anemia caught up with her quickly, and before she knew it she couldn't move.

But Kazuki took action before he even understood what was wrong. All he knew was that there was a girl collapsed in the road for some reason with tears streaming down her face. "What's wrong?" he asked.

"School..." the girl said.

"Wanna hop on?" he asked plainly. It hadn't occurred to him that doing such a thing would make him stand out far more than whatever it was he forgot to bring. All he was thinking about was getting home fast to retrieve his forgotten belongings and returning to school just as fast.

"I carried you, didn't I?"

"You gave me a lift," she corrected, her face still bright red.

She explained what had happened that day. He was nice enough to give her a lift, but she was afraid he might take her back to her house. Or, even worse, the hospital. The doctors would have been quite angry. She wondered anxiously if he was really taking her to school as she clung to his back.

Her anxiety soon changed to surprise and joy. This boy is amazing, she thought. The scenery seemed to be whipping by. Even with her on his back, his legs lunged out, struck the ground, and lunged out again at an incredible speed. So this is what it's like to run, she thought. She felt like bursting into laughter.

"Heh, I'm like a horse." Kazuki imagined some mangy carriage-puller.

"You're the prince's white horse," she corrected scoldingly. Wasn't it supposed to be the prince *on* a white horse? Well, either way, he was decidedly a horse. "Thanks to you, I was able to go to the opening assembly and surprise Maya, and I even felt a lot better. I managed to make it through fourth period, all the way to the end of the day. When I brought it up at home, my mom was surprised, too. She was a little angry, but she said she was glad, too," Shoko said this as if it was something truly incredible to her.

This was a refreshing shock to Kazuki. He never thought for a second that he had provided someone any kind of happiness. That he wasn't just hurting people. That he, who was swimming in the midst of a dark ocean, could have been somebody's light. He never would've believed it.

"In the Fafner, even I can run," Shoko whispered softly. "I can pay back my mother. For raising me." From her tone, it was clear that she understood what it meant to share her mother's blood. She was the opposite of Koyo, Kazuki thought. She was truly grateful to her mother.

"And I can be with you, too," she added, almost inaudibly. "But when the operation is over..."

"I'll get a bike," he blurted out. Shoko gave him a confused look.

"A bike?"

For someone like Kazuki, who could run forever without tiring himself out, who could walk for hours and not feel a hint of exhaustion, such a thing was unnecessary. But a bicycle really was faster than running, no matter how you looked at it.

"Isn't that what Tomi does?" he said. Once the island had migrated to a safe place and returned to peace, he would push his bike over to Shoko's house every morning just like Maya. On days Shoko could attend school, he would take her on the bike. On days that she couldn't, he would stay with her until class was about to start, then ride the bike to school.

He explained it all to her. It also occurred to him that this would allow him and Maya to go to school together, but he didn't bring it up.

"Really?" Shoko was so happy, she couldn't help but fear something terrible must be on the way, and her joy was mixed with anxiety.

She placed both hands on her heart. "Thank you, Kazuki-kun," she said, almost as if praying to God.

Suddenly, Kazuki felt terribly guilty about Koyo. For some reason, Maya popped into his mind. As he stood before a joyful, grinning Shoko, he was struck by a sense of distress. He recalled the sight of Soshi, yelling into a phone at some adult behind the school. He wondered if Soshi felt the same way now. From here on out, Kazuki and a great number of other pilots would be relying on his guidance. Looking back on Soshi trying desperately to help everyone evacuate the school, he had really taken on an incredibly heavy burden.

Please protect her. Koyo had said it, and Maya had, too. Surely they weren't just talking about Shoko. Surely they meant every single helpless person who stood behind those who were fighting.

Just as Kazuki had once seen an ocean of darkness floating behind Soshi's back, he now saw a faint cluster of lights behind Shoko. Lights coming from windows he couldn't enter.

Through Shoko, he knew that there were living presences in that light.

I will protect them.

The thought came out of nowhere. Maybe he

could really do it, he thought. That thing known as *peace*. It was one thing he would never hurt. He would use all of his strength to protect it.

Eventually, the pair reached the top of the slope. They stopped in front of an exquisite, Western-style house.

"I...I'll do my best to become the Mark Sechs pilot," Shoko said. "I'll work hard, and become like you." She sounded like she was clutching onto something for dear life.

The jet-black unit and pure white unit popped up in Kazuki's mind. Like light and dark, it was a partnership between two people who had gotten nothing out of their ordinary lives up until now.

"Yeah. Let's do it." He held out his hand. There was part of him that couldn't believe he was doing such a thing. As Shoko's face turned bright red again, shyly, like the time she waved at him from her window, she slowly reached for his hand and gripped it. He felt her slender fingers in the palm of his hand.

Let's protect this girl.

A very natural emotion bloomed inside him.

No matter what, I'll protect her.

He felt the strength of his conviction.

And such was the belief Kazuki held in his heart, before the days of peace truly came to an end.

Epilogue

I'll protect her.

In the blink of an eye, six months had passed since he made that vow.

He went on thinking he could protect her all along. He went on thinking he *had* to protect her. Forever. Even after he had already lost her.

This was because it was a promise he had made to the people most precious to him.

Kazuki felt himself returning to consciousness from his blanked-out state.

Where am I?

Setting questions aside, part of him unconsciously braced for pain. And in so doing, he recalled where he was.

It was the cockpit block.

"Your unit has just been secured in its cage on the dock. You'll be able to exit the cockpit soon," Soshi said as his red phantom image appeared in the darkness. Kazuki's consciousness became all the clearer.

Aha. He had been engaged in battle up until a bit ago. After defeating the enemy, Soshi had blanked his consciousness out of concern, and the autopilot had brought him back to the island.

He recalled the dreadful image of the destroyed "Yellow Coffin," the Mark Drei. Mark Vier had shot the assimilated Mark Drei's pilot.

Koyo the "Friend Killer."

He recalled that two pilots had fallen in battle. He had gotten Soshi to send their information, which he now began to recall.

"I dreamed about the past. Before I piloted a Fafner," he said softly.

The red-stained Soshi responded with a gentle smile. "I thought you looked peaceful."

"You were gathering the students together, yelling something behind the school, trying to get the entrance to Alvis open."

"Heh, did I do that? Feels like quite awhile ago."

"I thought so, too. Feels like it was years ago."

"You too, huh?"

"So, in my dream..."

"Yeah?"

"Shoko was there."

Shoshi narrowed his eyes. Both his right and his blind left eye.

"Quit blaming yourself, Kazuki."

" ...Right."

"Ejecting cockpit block."

" ...Okay."

At last, he rotated around vertically in his comfortable fetal position.

"So, Soshi. Who'd you bet on?" he asked before he was released back into the outside world.

"Hm? What do you mean?"

"My match, after school. You remember, right? With the other students. What about your bet?"

"Ah," Soshi nodded as it came back to him. His phantom image lost its connection and grew staticky. "Well, I...I forget."

Kazuki nodded. He had a feeling he'd say that. "Gotcha."

Soshi's image disappeared. Light came in its place. The cockpit block hatch had opened. Kazuki opened his eyes in a daze as he felt the light of the dock hit his face. He was struck by the usual uneasy feeling that accompanied release from his unified state with the Fafner. He endured it as he grabbed onto the extended hand of a maintenance worker and exited the cockpit.

Hadn't he been gripping a more slender hand?

His memories from the dream mixed with reality. He stood on the shiny, polished floor of the dock looking up at his Mark Elf unit, which had been destroyed in battle, and gradually took in reality. He unconsciously began looking around for a pure white unit, but stopped before considering what that meant.

"Well, you've torn it to bits again, eh, Crusher?" the maintenance worker laughed.

"Crusher" was the nickname the maintenance workers had given Kazuki. He had the highest rate of damage for both units and weapons (as well as the top enemy annihilation rate), and this was their way of being friendly with him. No matter how much he smashed up the units, they never complained.

Kazuki scanned the dock in a daze. He could

recall his fear and anxiety the first time he stood here. For the first time in a while, his emotions from before he knew the true meaning of the word *war* came back to him. It seemed traces of them still lingered in his heart.

Just how many times had he been in battle since then?

He stood pondering the question as the maintenance worker patted him on the shoulder.

"You bagged your forty-first enemy today. The runner-up is Mark Vier with sixteen. Pretty darn incredible, I gotta say. So should I throw some stars up on the Mark Elf's leg?"

"Stars?"

"You know, for show."

Eventually he grasped the meaning. The man wanted to put some star-shaped marks on the leg of the Fafner to indicate how many enemies he had destroyed, so that Kazuki could show it off to everyone. The man seemed to think Kazuki would really like the idea. Everyone was so happy Kazuki had returned alive, and they were grateful to him for fighting.

But Kazuki refused. "No, thanks."

"You sure?"

"I'd end up with stars all over my body. Just keep it black, please." He wasn't being boastful. He really intended to keep crushing the enemy for as long as he lived, killing hundreds upon hundreds.

"Point taken." The maintenance man gave Kazuki a hearty grin and another rough pat on the shoulder.

Kazuki went off to the Changing Room without

even so much as a nod.

A voice came from behind. "You ought to go ahead and stick some on. Stars, I mean." It was a cold, thorny, challenging voice. "How else is a guy like you supposed to keep track of how many units he's destroyed? Just think of them as a sort of reminder."

Slowly, Kazuki turned to face the speaker.

"I'm not looking to play around with my unit, Koyo."

"Haha. You've gotta be a little playful in a world like this, Ace," Koyo laughed scornfully. "It's a war, after all."

What the hell is this guy talking about? Kazuki seriously thought for a moment. It was probably because he had been thinking about when things were peaceful. The thought that the Koyo from the old days, before he ever entered a Fafner, would never have said such a thing floated through Kazuki's mind for a moment, and then disappeared.

Without saying anything else, Kazuki started to leave.

"Do you know what 'Festum' means?" Koyo asked, coming closer.

"Search me." He had never even thought about it. Why they called the enemy that had nothing to do with him.

"Unlike you, I sweat the small stuff." Koyo gave a very showy shrug of his shoulders and paused for a moment. "'Festival'," he said, snickering to himself. "They've come here to celebrate with us, all shiny and glittering. They figure all this fighting is fun."

"Fun?"

"Yup. That's what those ten rings are for." Koyo spread his hands out and showed them. There were bruises around the bases of his fingers. Marks left by the rings—they were what immediately separated pilots from non-pilots, veterans from rookies. They were the meaning of the pilots' existence. They were the artificially created stigmata that brought forth the gifted pilots' most violent urges.

But Kazuki's eyes were focused on Koyo's cold grin. He felt like he was realizing for the first time that the old Koyo who always accepted him with gentle warmth was no longer in this world. Surely this was also because he had been thinking about the past.

This time he began to leave for real. As he turned his back on Koyo, he heard him whisper something.

"Kazuki...next time I'll be the one to defeat more. Someday, I'll beat you. I'll prove to everybody that I'm the better pilot. Lone Dog son of a bitch."

Spurred by that final insult, Kazuki felt the urge to turn back around.

Lone Dog—battle via a single unit. One of the most strictly prohibited actions of a pilot. Having convinced Soshi to give him permission, it was one of Kazuki's few consolations in life. Soshi had convinced the adults for him. It was the last refuge for Kazuki after losing his partner.

He headed to the Changing Room in silence. Koyo went to join his friends and began laughing boisterously about something.

Ocean Baseball—suddenly it popped into

Kazuki's mind. It felt like a lifetime ago. But it also felt like part of him hadn't changed since then. He was just doing as told to the best of his ability; no more, no less. Consequently, no matter how much everyone else managed to lose themselves in the thrill of the game, for him it was impossible.

He removed his suit and changed into his own clothes. He proceeded to the Bahnzweck and boarded it alone.

Staring blankly into the dark ocean, he remembered Kuramae. Then Shoko. Then all of the many people he had lost.

He shed no tears. Nor could he laugh like Koyo. He just stared into the dark, undulating ocean in silence.

He exited the Bahnzweck and began making his way through the tunnels of Alvis.

Midway through, he suddenly felt the urge to switch paths. He went all the way back the way he had come and entered an elevator. The paths he once couldn't remember were now reasonably deducible from the string of letters and numbers running through his mind.

Why was he doing this?

It must have been because he had been remembering the beginning of the war. Back before he knew true loss. When he still believed he could protect others.

As he reflected on this, he came to the path

he was looking for and ascended a flight of stairs. He opened a panel placed by a barrier. He produced a black card and inserted it into the lower part of the panel, then began to operate it. Soon enough, the barrier opened, freeing the way. Kazuki put the card away and went outside.

His eyes were filled with lush greenery. Between the trees, he could make out the coastline of what was still known to this day as the "Western Slope."

What was he doing here?

What was supposed to be here?

He stared out at the scenery.

"Kazuki...kun?" someone called. His eyes widened. He spun around in surprise. It was Maya. "What are you doing in a place like this?"

"That's my line."

It felt like this was the first time he had seen Maya in ages, but since she was serving in the battle command post, she probably had seen him in battle, he reckoned. But he never knew where she was at such times.

Kazuki had mostly stopped going to school. The pilots were gradually losing the spare time to even show up to first period to be with everyone else. At this point, he only managed to go about once every two weeks, and even then, he would usually feel extremely uncomfortable as soon as he sat down in the classroom and always ended up leaving the building.

Everybody at school knew Kazuki was an ace pilot. And Kazuki knew that many of the students were placing bets on him. On how many enemies he would defeat—or if he would be defeated. He didn't know the maximum bet. Maybe two thousand.

It was only on the sparse occasions when he talked to Maya that he could really feel at ease. He realized this every time she appeared before him.

And this time was no different. He was glad that he had come here today, from the bottom of his heart.

"I come here quite a bit after work."

"Oh."

"You too, Kazuki?"

"No. Today's my first time."

Maya nodded, as if she had already known just by looking at his face.

They stood together, looking at the scenery from the hill.

The first tank they had seen, the world crumbling to pieces, all of it started here.

He glanced over at Maya's profile. She was completely absorbed in viewing the scenery, as told by her innocent gaze.

Was it possible that her awareness restriction code was still at the lowest level? She viewed the completely changed world with such distance in her eyes that it really did seem possible. Or maybe it was just Kazuki's wish. He didn't bother trying to ask her. Nor did he ask her how she saw him. Something about it was daunting.

"We went from here to meet Shoko, didn't we? All of us together," she said softly.

It was the first time Kazuki had heard Maya say that name in ages. He felt a pang in his heart. Whether it was because she knew how much it hurt him, or because it hurt her even more, Maya rarely ever spoke of Shoko anymore.

"After we lost Shoko, I finally understood how she felt for the first time. I mean, I'm not a pilot. I can't even remember anything about Alvis. I'm just baggage. Just hearing the word 'Alvis' fills me with a weird feeling I don't think I'll ever get over."

So that *was* the case. Kazuki suppressed the urge to say so, and kept his mouth shut. Surely *this* was what Maya felt was her real handicap. While everyone else was rapidly adapting to the wartime regime, she was too afraid to even board the Bahnzweck.

"I can't do anything. I'm just watching everyone. I never would've thought it would be so painful. It's worthless to just say you understand people's feelings. If I can't put myself in their shoes, I'm just worthless."

Hearing Maya's sullen voice, Kazuki felt like he might really lose his mind. Still, he was only able to respond with a silent nod.

Speaking of abilities, all Kazuki could do was get inside a Fafner and put a few more inches of distance between the island and peril. If that seemed like a big deal, it was worth taking a harder look at Maya's true role, to see how she spoke to those who had suffered the grief of lost relatives, to those who were bed-ridden from terrible wounds, to those who had contracted incurable diseases during their research in Alvis. It was worth seeing how she put their hearts at ease.

And just as her presence had come to these people's rescue, so, too, had she come to Kazuki's. To

him, she was the far more amazing one.

He still remembered when she told him not to go with Soshi. When she had stopped them from leaving the school together. It wasn't that he regretted becoming a Fafner pilot. It was just that her words from that day seemed to somehow keep him tied to something precious, even now, long after he had chosen to pilot.

"Rabbit..." Kazuki randomly blurted out.

"Huh?" Maya turned and looked at him.

Raking through his memory, he recalled that this too had been one of her words.

"Do you remember? Before Kuramae and I made our way through this tunnel to the Bahnzweck, you said that to Soshi. 'Rabbit.'"

"Yeah, I remember." She smiled, as if thankfully surprised that *he* had remembered. "At that time, I thought Soshi-kun was going to eat you up."

"Eat...me?"

"Rabbits eat their babies sometimes, right? Like if a human touches one. I don't know if it's because the smell of human sticks or because they don't want the humans to take the babies away, but I thought he was going to try to eat up the thing most precious to him in order to protect it. Not just Soshi, but you too, and everyone else. That's how it seemed, anyway."

"To protect the most precious thing?"

Maya was being terribly depressing. Kazuki became all the more unable to respond with anything but nods.

"And somehow I knew that was the only choice. And I knew that you'd probably go on your own. After that first battle...I was so glad you were alive. I was so thankful that you were still you."

"Maybe I was eaten, really," Kazuki said softly.

Eaten by what, exactly?

The war, no doubt. It had eaten the lives and hearts of so many.

He thought of Koyo. The completely changed face of he who was once a friend. Koyo with his gentle smile, who left no consideration unattended to, who was truly delighted by the sight of two people getting along. But he had lost the Mark Sechs, received the nickname of "Friend Killer," and seen so many precious things fade away one by one.

With that in mind, Kazuki couldn't help but think, *I'm fine.* Just as he had always thought, before the war as well as now. It was how he kept himself going.

Nobody blamed Kazuki for the loss of Mark Sechs. Nobody would give him that satisfaction.

That is, except for Koyo. Even now, Koyo continued to resent him, convinced that if it had been him instead of Kazuki, he could've protected Mark Sechs. In trying to prove that, he strove to beat Kazuki— and rapidly changed.

"They'll be doing construction work here eventually, they say," Maya said in a whisper. "It's going to change. Everything. Not just here, but all over the place, we'll be losing forests to make way for weapons to defeat the enemy. It's like they're trying to forget the old days as fast as they can."

"Will you remember me?" Kazuki asked, praying in his heart that she shared his feelings. His question was like a precious object being passed to the listener. If it were damaged, there would be no recovery. It was that precious.

Maya received the question as if wrapping herself around it. "You bet I will. I always have," she said as if it should've been obvious.

"Are you...glad I'm here," Kazuki asked.

It was a strange question. Maybe he really wanted to be asking Soshi, Kuramae, Koyo—and Shoko.

But Maya understood that *this* question was the real precious object. "I am," she said. "Thank you for being here." There was a brief pause. "And it's not because you've beaten so many enemies," she said.

Kazuki felt like he could cry right then and there. Like Kuramae, he could turn his back to Maya, softly wiping his eyes.

But he did not.

Her sweet voice was incredibly soothing. He felt that if he could just keep listening to that voice forever that would be enough. He couldn't possibly want for anything more. Likely, that was one light he had left behind when he began swimming into the dark ocean.

With that, the pair made their way down the hill to the road leading home. Because the island kept moving around, the sun was in a different place every time they thought to look. Maya looked up at the sky, shielding her eyes with her hand.

"I...I think I get why the enemy asks that question," she said with a tinge of humor mixed in.

"Question?" Kazuki realized what she was

referring to as he spoke. The question posed by the Sphinx model enemy. The question that bored its way into your heart, trying to control your entire being.

Are you there?

But it seemed Maya had a different answer than Kazuki.

"They probably really don't know."

"Don't know?"

"Humans are a strange breed. Even if they're 'there,' you don't know if they're *really* there. Sometimes there's not really a person there at all, and that person is off in a completely different place," Maya said. "So, Kazuki-kun? Are *you* there?" she said to the one who was really there by her side.

"Yeah...And it feels like it's the first time in a while," he answered with a slight shrug.

"Hehe. I see, I see." Maya did a little hop. "That's good," she said as she landed. Somehow her motion seemed to serve as an acknowledgment that they were both there.

Kazuki felt his feet naturally turn him towards the sea. It probably meant something slightly different than when Kuramae had turned her heels on him. Maybe he just wanted to make sure this peaceful feeling was real.

"Kazuki-kun?"

"I'm gonna make a quick stop before I go home."

"Oh. Okay. See you." She gave him an energetic wave.

Kazuki nodded and began on his way again.

"Hey, Kazuki-kun?" she said with just a hint of melancholy. She checked to make sure he had stopped completely before she spoke. "Come back sometimes, okay?"

Kazuki listened to her voice in silence. That sweet voice he wanted to go on listening to forever.

"Because I'll always be here."

Most likely alone, here on this island.

She would be here, never forgetting those days of peace.

She would go on protecting them.

In Maya's heart, a great number of people went on living, smiling even now.

For the first time in a long time, Kazuki could feel his face naturally curl into a grin.

"I'll come back...sometimes. To wherever you are."

Maya nodded and waved once again, this time gently.

Kazuki made his way down to the beach and walked along the coast. The rhythmic sound of the crashing waves fell over him. And with it, the feeling that he might cry faded.

He walked along the beach until, out of nowhere, he spotted a piece of something washed up on the shore. He halted in his tracks.

The depressing notion that it could have been a chunk of the Mark Sechs occurred to him. After waging a fierce battle, the white unit had been obliterated, leaving not a single trace. It wouldn't be right to go searching for its remains. Shoko had said it herself.

She who had been born wrong would return to the earth, praying that next time she would come out correctly. She would find peace in imagining herself scattering into a million particles of dust. She had told him so herself. And Shoko had become exactly as she said. All he could do now was pray together with her. That was his role. That was his limit.

He cast his eyes away from the piece and resumed walking. As he did so, he discovered that unidentifiable fragments had washed up all over the beach. Perhaps they belonged to a unit someone had been riding in. Maybe machine and pilot had burst apart in the same moment, sending pieces to where Kazuki now stood.

"It's a war, after all." Koyo's words came back to him. He stopped in his tracks again.

Get real.

He clenched his fists and glared up into the sky. The rage filling his heart was not something to direct at Koyo. It was directed at everything that had made Koyo say that. At everything that had made the Koyo he knew disappear. At the enormous beast known as war which greedily devoured hearts and lives. At everything in the entire world, including himself. He wanted to scream it.

Get real.

As they all went on wounding each other's precious things. As they fought over those things that, once lost, never come back. As they somehow went on living. They were all *there.*

He thought of crying. But no tears would come. He guessed he must have still been fine. Either that, or he was going to lose his mind. Unable to shed even a single tear, he felt severely betrayed. He forced himself to put one foot forward, and then resumed walking once again.

Surely the topic of betting on how many enemies he had defeated would come up again around the same time tomorrow. Some would win and some would lose as they placed their bets in a place he didn't know, unaware that he intended to go on crushing the enemy by the hundreds and thousands.

Thinking about the bets, he remembered something. It wasn't related to any battle. It was back during the days of peace. Who had Soshi bet on? Recalling his voice from when he claimed to have forgotten, Kazuki thought of something else. Perhaps Soshi never even placed a bet. Kazuki had never considered that possibility before. But perhaps Soshi had only said that as a warning to make Kazuki stop being foolish. Maybe Soshi was irritated by the way Kazuki had passively allowed himself to become the subject of other people's gambling. But this was all conjecture, and Kazuki was never good at making deductions based on circumstantial evidence.

Somehow the thought made him want to apologize, want to laugh out loud. It was a strange feeling.

What a joke, he snickered.

Suddenly he felt fulfilled. He came to a stop yet again, and this time it was for sure.

Let's leave this island.

The thought rose up from the depths of his heart. This, too, was likely because he was remembering the days of peace. "One more year," he had said to Koyo. In one more year, he would leave the island and go someplace where no one knew him.

Casually, he scanned the sky. "Ahh..." A sigh spilled out. The sun was in a familiar place. Because the island had migrated, because it had fled in search of Peace, at some point East and West had returned to their positions from before the fighting began.

What a wonder, he thought. Everything had come full circle from the day the island sun set in the east and April 1st became the end of September. It was just like a Fafner pilot floating like a fetus inside the cockpit, returning to his original weighted state; the sun had returned to its proper place before he even realized it.

In the end, it was all a lie, he thought as he stared at the sun. *I'm fine,* he always said. It was a lie. He was tired of hurting and being hurt. He didn't want to hurt anybody. Not even the enemy. He wanted to beg them to stop hurting as well. That was the truth. He wanted to run from the fighting and leave the island. Anywhere was fine. He wanted to go to a place he didn't know and where no one knew him. Of course he knew it was a meaningless wish. If he took even one step outside, he would enter an ever-expanding world of death where no one would come to his aid.

Still, one day he would go. One day. When the island had finally arrived at a place of Peace. When he had carried out his promise to protect everyone. And when he finally did leave the island, he might even think to come back some day. Maybe the true him was there somewhere.

When there's peace, that's what I'll do.

As he affirmed it in his mind, he thought of the word *bicycle*. That's right, he had told Shoko he would buy a bicycle when there was peace. The memory came back to him out of nowhere. He imagined himself riding his bicycle through the crumbled world, feeling good. He could feel the soothing wind grazing by his face. It was a terribly comforting, irresistible daydream. Even if it was completely detached from reality. Or rather, *because* it was.

When peace returns once again, I'll go through this destroyed world on the bicycle I never ended up getting.

As he affirmed it in his mind and looked up into the sky—

A single tear ran down.

He gasped at it as it emerged, as if to sew together the hole in his heart. Cautiously, he raised a hand to his eye to make sure it was really there.

A moment before he could touch it—

That which had come from a place that transcended any and every intention slowly tricked down his dry cheek, wetting it along the way.

He just watched the sky. Looking into the vast, expansive blue, he thought about how it was like seeing the sun from the middle of a dark ocean. The next thing he knew, he was on his knees.

In the pit of his stomach, he heard the voice he had been hoping for, calling out. It didn't stop. Could it be that the real him that he thought he'd lost was there? Had the self that had been hidden away finally arrived at a safe place and come forth?

Like it mattered.

Someone was there. That was all. Whether he was truly fine or not, he was finally able to cry out loud in all its disgracefulness. *Someone*—made just a little bit sad by his lack of a place in the world—was there.

Afterword

Adios! Nice-to-meet-you people and fancy-seeing-you-here people alike, good afternoon! Ubukata Tow, here.

First, a word about this work of fiction. This here is the novelized version of the television anime "Soukyuu no Fafner," which I, after receiving the consent of various concerned parties to do whatever the heck I wanted with, wrote in an entirely self-indulgent manner. It's the Ubukata Tow version, if you will.

As it would happen, the editing department, upon discovering the words "Soukyuu no Fastener (Zipper)" written on the manuscript (a draft submitted before publishing used to check for various errors), had a bit of a self-indulgence fest of their own, launching a pinpoint assault on me. There sat your beloved author, partially fueled on an all-nighter's high, laughing to the point of breathing problems. Come to think of it, there was also a certain notorious, alleged womanizer of a "Middle-West Producer" heard to be drunkenly raving about "Soukyuu no Fastener!" on a certain radio program. Mistakes abound if you let your guard down. "We can't run an adult program like that! What do you *mean* it's already out?"

Anywho.

It came to be that I, the humble novelist Ubukata,

was to become the literary overseer for "Soukyuu no Fafner."

I still remember it. The very first business meeting. The famous King Records' producer, known to the world as "Middle-West," sitting beside the famous producer "Big Moon," who said very succinctly,

"There's no time!!"

Bang. Fist on table.

Never before or since have I felt less of a will to raise an argument.

And this was our first meeting. At this point, I wasn't even aware that he had produced "Evangelion." At any rate, being the complete amateur that I was in the world of anime production, I couldn't be expected to know exactly why there was no time or what particular time he was referring to, but at any rate the sense of a fast-approaching time limit was thick in the air.

What was proposed that day was a show that had "robots, an island, and a character-driven plot." As if it had all been predestined, I still remember how the idea of how to make all of that into a story naturally came to us. Most likely, Kazuki, Soshi, Maya, and the others were already looking to be born somewhere in the world, and they just happened to choose me as the first available opportunity to do so.

And so it was that—thanks to the sensibilities, skills, and knowledge of a variety of individuals—a cast of characters, their town, their lives, and their battles became elaborately fleshed out, one right after another. In all of that, I was nothing more than a single member of a staff. I was fortunate to have the opportunity to experience such an enjoyable, exciting production.

As this and that were going on, it turned out that I was to be in charge of writing the scenarios. Still, that really just meant going to Kazuki and the others for answers.

What kind of life are you trying to live, and through what mindset?

So asking, I somehow managed to fish the answers out of them, and then it was just a matter of writing them down as accurately as my own ability would allow. What's more, it wasn't simply me working alone, but a task encompassed by the almost unbelievably tremendous efforts and considerations of a great many staff members. They graciously corrected all those answers I had misheard, allowing me to entirely rewrite them.

Meanwhile, this novel being a collection of answers given by Kazuki and the others, there are various points that differ from what you may have seen in the anime. *But,* I would be very much obliged if you would think of it as two different sides to the same answer. It should be realized, even after experiencing both the novel and the anime, that I haven't done anything particularly special. Kazuki and the others were born very much autonomously and then just hung on to life for all it was worth, and all I'm doing is constantly praying that maybe they'll be loved by one more person.

Well, we've reached the end, but please allow me to renew my thanks and acknowledgements.

I owe a great deal of gratitude to Middle-West

Producer-san. He provided me with an immense amount of advice while I was getting the ball rolling, and for that I am truly in his debt.

To "Yu"-san, who received me with a cheerful smile even when I was coming dangerously close to not meeting the deadline, I owe a great deal—and I do mean a *great* deal—of thanks. I don't know whether you were smiling on the phone as well, but...you were, right? Right?

An enormous thanks to Hirai-san, who, under an enormous pile of work, went to the extra effort to draw me a full-color leaflet (!) for the front of this book. Including the front binding, he did nearly ten pictures in all. That's enough art to bind several anime magazines now, honestly.

Thanks to the many, many individuals who contributed their labors to "Soukyuu no Fafner"—the director, producers, and everyone else. I enjoyed much excitement, enlightenment, and delight.

And finally...

To all the viewers and readers out there who have shown Kazuki and the others your love.

Really, thank you so much.

I humbly beseech your continued support for our beloved friends, from now until forever.

November, 2004
Tow Ubukata

Minoru Murao 2006. First published in 2006 by Media Works Inc., Tokyo, Japan. English translation rights arranged with Media Works Inc.

A LESSON IN
Foreign Relations

RED

レッド

BY
SANAE ROKUYA
ISBN#978-156970-714-2
$12.95

Available Now!

TAIYOH TOSHO

www.taiyo-pub.co.jp

June

junemanga.com